HOW TO PROTECT YOU
KF 510 B52

DATE DUE

JY 25 '96			
MR 12 '97			
OC 27 '03			

DEMCO 38-296

How to Protect Your Spousal Rights

TOM BIRACREE

CB
CONTEMPORARY
BOOKS
CHICAGO

Riverside Community College
Library
4800 Magnolia Avenue
Riverside, California 92506

JUN '93

Library of Congress Cataloging-in-Publication Data

Biracree, Tom, 1947-
How to protect your spousal rights : the complete guide to your legal and financial rights / Tom Biracree.
p. cm.
"An American information book"—T.p. verso.
Includes index.
ISBN 0-8092-3972-8 (pbk.)
1. Husband and wife—United States. 2. Women—Legal status, laws, etc.—United States. 3. Equitable distribution of marital property—United States. 4. Support (Domestic relations)—United States. 5. Windows—Legal status, laws, etc.—United States. I. Title.
KF510.B525 1991
346.7301'63—dc20 91-23040
[347.306163] CIP

An American Information Book
Copyright © 1991 by Tom Biracree
All rights reserved
Published by Contemporary Books, Inc.
180 North Michigan Avenue, Chicago, Illinois 60601
Manufactured in the United States of America
International Standard Book Number: 0-8092-3972-8

Contents

Introduction

When you made plans to marry, your thoughts probably were concentrated on the love and the happiness that you and your fiancé planned to derive from a life that you would make together. You may not have taken time to reflect that you were entering into a new legal status. This special status reflects the state's belief in the importance of marriage as a social institution. Although entering into marriage is strictly voluntary, neither you nor your spouse are free to determine many of the rules by which your marriage will be conducted nor can you unilaterally decide when and how the marriage will end. From the moment you say "I do," both you and your spouse incur certain duties, liabilities, rights, and privileges.

In the romantic glow of those immediate pre- and post-wedding days, the legal rights and responsibilities of marriage don't seem very important. Unfortunately, reality eventually sets in. About half of all marriages today end in divorce. If you are a woman, chances are nine out of ten that you eventually will become a widow. You and your spouse are likely to have children, buy a home, assume debts, make investments, open retirement accounts, take out insurance policies, etc. All these acts incur special legal implications because you are married. In today's complex world, you must protect yourself—as well as your children and your spouse—by fully understanding your rights during and after marriage.

WHAT IS A MARRIAGE?

Under English common law, on which American law is based, a marriage is a voluntary union for life of one man and one woman, to the exclusion of all others. In recent years, every state has enacted laws that make ending a marriage less difficult. To date, however, no state has legalized same-sex marriages.

Although the decision to marry is voluntary, every state has established criteria to determine if a union constitutes a legal marriage and has set forth procedures that must be followed by the marrying couple. Among these criteria are:

- The marrying couple must not have certain family relationships to each other. Marriages between blood relatives, such as parent and child, siblings, and aunt/uncle and nephew/niece, are not allowed. Many states ban marriages between first cousins. Some states also prohibit marriages between family members by marriage, such as stepparent and stepchild, stepsiblings, or sister-in-law and brother-in-law.
- Both the man and the woman must be able to marry. That is, they must be legally unmarried and, to the best of their knowledge, able to consummate the marriage.
- Both the man and the woman must consent to the marriage. All states establish a legal age of consent, with under-age marriages deemed invalid. Many states also prohibit severely mentally retarded and mentally ill people from marrying because they are deemed incapable of understanding the implications of marriage.
- Both the man and the woman must be free of venereal disease and certain other medical conditions.

- Both the man and the woman must be willing to marry. A marriage isn't valid if either party is coerced or under the influence of alcohol or drugs.
- Both the man and the woman must intend to stay married for life. Marriages of convenience that are entered into for immigration or other reasons are not valid.

Some of the procedures required to become legally married are designed to ensure that some of these criteria are met. For example, to obtain a marriage license, couples must prove that they are of legal age and are not illegally related and that they have been legally divorced if they previously were married. Most states require blood tests for venereal diseases. Most states also require a waiting period between issuing a license and performing the marriage ceremony to discourage impulsive marriages and to allow objections to be raised.

Fourteen states (Alabama, Colorado, Georgia, Idaho, Iowa, Kansas, Montana, Ohio, Oklahoma, Pennsylvania, Rhode Island, South Carolina, Texas, and Utah) and the District of Columbia recognize "common-law" marriages. The difference between a common-law marriage and cohabitation is that a common-law marriage requires that a couple consider themselves married and present themselves as husband and wife. Most couples cohabit as an alternative to marriage. Although criteria for common-law marriages vary from state to state, the most common are using the same last name, referring to each other as husband and wife, filing joint income tax returns, opening joint bank accounts, and listing both names on the birth certificate of their children. If a couple meets the criteria for being married by common law in one state, they still are considered legally married if they move to a state that doesn't recognize common-law marriages. Children of common-law marriages are considered legitimate and both spouse and children have the legal right of inheritance. Even though common-law marriages take place outside of the legal system, they can be ended only through the same divorce proceedings required of couples who were married legally.

Almost all states have laws that protect one or both spouses who honestly and reasonably believe that they are married, even though the marriage may not be valid. One example of what is called a "putative" marriage is a ceremony performed by a clergyman who, unbeknownst to the couple, did not have the proper legal authority. This couple would be considered legally married under the law even without going through another ceremony. A spouse who discovers that his or her marriage wasn't legal because the other spouse wasn't legally divorced also is given considerable protections, including the right to inherit, the right to a property settlement, the right to have children of the relationship declared legitimate, and the right to seek child support.

WHY IS IT SO IMPORTANT TO UNDERSTAND WHAT A MARRIAGE IS?

For centuries, marriage was a legally simple relationship. A husband exercised total control over his wife, all her property, and the children. In return, he was solely responsible for supporting the family. In today's complex society, however, a marriage represents a dramatic and complex change in legal status. For example, the rule of thumb "what's mine is mine, what's yours is yours" instantly changes. Almost all of your income becomes marital property, some of which may be used by your spouse and all of which may be distributed by the courts if the marriage is ended.

You also acquire a right to marital privacy, which most people understand to mean the right to engage in sexual relations. Marital privacy, however, also removes from court supervision such activities as the financial relationship between husband and wife. One member of a cohabiting couple can legally enforce a contract that requires the other member to purchase a new car. But the courts would not enforce the same contract between husband and wife.

At a time when two-income couples are the rule rather than the exception, marriage also gives each spouse complex obligations to support each other and any children that they may have. Failure to understand these obligations can produce unpleasant surprises during and after the marriage.

As a result, you should not enter into a marriage or live in a marriage without thoroughly understanding your legal rights and responsibilities. This book provides a complete explanation of how you can protect yourself by:

- Negotiating a prenuptial agreement
- Managing your money properly
- Understanding your joint tax benefits and liabilities
- Safeguarding your Social Security and pension benefits
- Planning your estate and preparing a will
- Guarding against domestic violence
- Understanding your children's rights
- Following the proper procedures when divorcing
- Enforcing court orders after a divorce
- Preparing before entering into a remarriage
- Preparing for becoming a widow or widower

1

The Prenuptial Agreement

KEY FACTS

- A prenuptial agreement is a contract in which you and your spouse give up certain rights or take on certain responsibilities, primarily financial, that otherwise would not be provided for in the marital laws of your state.
- Prenuptial agreements are desirable when one or both partners have significant assets or children by a previous marriage or own a business.
- Prenuptial agreements must meet strict legal standards that are designed to protect against premarital coercion or deception.

Even with divorce rates reaching upward of 50 percent of all marriages, you and your fiancé, along with many other couples, may view the signing of a legal agreement before marriage as "cold" and "unromantic." As mentioned in the introduction to this book, however, marriage is a legal institution as well as a social status in which both you and your future spouse assume new rights and responsibilities. A prenuptial agreement is a practical way to deal with some of these rights and responsibilities. An agreement is just as important as deciding on the purchase of a home, taking out life insurance, or drawing up a will. A prenuptial agreement does not increase the likelihood of you and your spouse divorcing. In fact, you may find that discussing such sensitive subjects brings you even closer together, and coming to an agreement eliminates certain fears and worries that can cause problems months or years after you say "I do."

DO YOU NEED THE PROTECTION OF A PRENUPTIAL AGREEMENT?

When couples are about to marry, they make many promises to each other. Because marriage is accorded such a special status by the law, however, state courts will enforce only a few types of promises, those that are made in strict accordance with certain rules and procedures. Generally, these types of promises involve what almost every couple finds to be a very touchy subject: the disposition of financial assets and responsibilities that one or both partners bring to a marriage in the event that the union ends in death, separation, or divorce. Although you may be reluctant to think about these unpleasant eventualities when you are basking in the happiness of your engagement, you must realize that a legally valid prenuptial agreement is the *only* way to ensure that financial promises are kept.

Couples who marry young, before either person has had a chance to accumulate significant assets or take on significant financial responsibilities, have little need for a formal prenuptial agreement. If, however, you have been working for a number of years before marriage or if you are marrying for the second time, you should take the following quiz. If your answer to any of these questions is yes, you would very likely benefit from a prenuptial agreement.

California Marriage Law

Ed Sherman

Prenups for Lovers: A Romantic Guide to Prenup.

Arlene G Dubin

UCR.edu

— Do I have significant assets, such as a house, investments, pension funds, jewelry, furniture, a vacation home, or life insurance?
— Does my future spouse have such assets?
— Do I own a business, a share in a business or partnership, patents, or copyrights?
— Does my future spouse own a business, a share in a business or partnership, patents, or copyrights?
— Do I have at least one person who is financially dependent on me, such as a child or parent?
— Does my future spouse have at least one person who is financially dependent on him or her?

WHAT PRENUPTIAL AGREEMENTS CANNOT COVER

A prenuptial agreement can contain anything you and your spouse want to include in it. But state courts generally will not enforce provisions in the following areas:

1. Marital privacy. Except in extreme circumstances, such as abandonment, abuse, and fraud, states will not interfere in the way married couples lead their daily lives. For example, a court won't enforce agreements that spell out who will take out the garbage, the religion in which children will be raised, the allowance one spouse gives to the other for household expenses, how much money can be spent on travel or clothing, and a host of similar issues. A court also will not enforce "open-marriage" agreements that state one spouse will not charge another with adultery in the case of an affair.

The only exceptions to this rule are provisions for meeting certain obligations that existed prior to a marriage. For instance, one spouse may agree to pay half the mortgage on the house in which the couple lives or to pay a fixed monthly sum toward the support of a child from a previous marriage.

2. Support or custody of the children. Courts will not let a couple decide before marriage about who will get custody of the children born of the marriage or how much support these children will receive in the event of a divorce.

3. Divorce settlement. Courts also will not enforce certain provisions in the settlement in the event of a divorce. This will be discussed in detail later in this chapter.

WHAT ARE THE REQUIREMENTS FOR A BINDING PRENUPTIAL AGREEMENT?

Going through the sometimes delicate process of negotiating and signing a prenuptial agreement is a waste of time if any of the provisions turn out to be unenforceable in court. To protect yourself and your dependents, you must make sure that you meet the following requirements set forth by most state courts:

1. Your agreement must be in writing. Verbal agreements are nearly impossible to enforce in every state. Some states require that written prenuptial agreements must be recorded at city or county clerks' offices to be valid.

2. *Both* you and your future spouse should hire your own attorneys to represent you. Because the specific financial circumstances of couples and the laws of each state vary so widely, do-it-yourself prenuptial agreements are extremely unwise. Trying to save money on legal expenses inevitably will result in much higher expenses should the marriage end.

But why do we need separate attorneys? you may ask. For two reasons. First, before a judge will enforce your prenuptial agreement, he or she must be convinced that both you and your spouse fully and completely understood the implications of every provision. Among the circumstances that may raise doubt are:

- To save money on legal expenses, you asked your brother-in-law to draw up the agreement.

- Your future spouse wanted the agreement drawn up by the firm that does the legal work for his business because of the firm's detailed knowledge of his finances.

Although a fair agreement may result in both cases, the circumstances may create an appearance of bias that may void the agreement. If you and your future spouse do share an attorney, make sure you hire an impartial professional with no prior ties to either of you.

Second, many couples find that directly negotiating the details of a prenuptial agreement is extremely stressful. You may end up with a better agreement at a lower emotional cost by letting your attorneys negotiate the specific language of the contract.

3. You and your future spouse must fully disclose all your financial assets, obligations, and responsibilities. Nothing voids a prenuptial agreement more quickly than proof that one spouse withheld any information about assets, ownership in businesses, debts, or other relevant subjects. The requirement for you and your spouse to disclose what you have and what you owe isn't limited to obvious things, such as bank accounts, stocks and bonds, property, or credit-card debts. Rather, it includes everything that contributes to your net worth. For example:

- Your spouse is a serious stamp collector who values her collection at the price that she paid for the stamps. She fails to tell you that the present worth of the collection is 10 or 20 times that amount, and that the proceeds of buying and selling stamps represent a significant portion of her income.
- You fail to inform your spouse that half the proceeds from the sale of your house (in which you are going to live) will go to your ex-spouse under the provisions of the divorce agreement.

It's important to understand that each spouse has the right to complete knowledge of the other spouse's net worth, even if specific assets (such as ownership of a stamp collection) aren't part of the prenuptial agreement. The best way to do this is for you and your future spouse to prepare individual net-worth statements.

Your net worth is the result of subtracting what you owe from what you have. Your assets may include:

- cash
- bank balances
  - checking
  - savings
  - certificates of deposit
- savings bonds
- bonds
- life insurance cash value
- mutual funds
- other investments
- retirement plans
- private pension funds
- profit-sharing plans
- market value of home
- other real estate
- equity in a business
- cars
- household goods
- collections
- debts others owe you

Your liabilities may include:

- current bills
- mortgage debt
- credit-card and installment debt
- taxes due
- debts owed others
- child support or alimony
- student loans
- business loans

Some of this information, such as the balances in your bank accounts, is readily available. Other information, such as the current value of your home, your business, or your stamp collection, probably requires some investigation.

You can use a simple ledger sheet or a pad of paper to compute your net worth. You may, however, want to use the worksheets and information from the following sources:

▶ **Handbook:** *Managing Your Personal Finances*
Cost: $6.50 per set
Contains: An extremely valuable and useful three-part series on personal finance and financial planning prepared by the Extension Service of the U.S. Department of Agriculture. The three parts are:

1. The Principles of Managing your Finances
2. Financial Tools Used in Money Management
3. Coping with Change

These sections are hole-punched to fit a three-hole binder, so that the many worksheets included are removable for your calculations.
From: Superintendent of Documents
Government Printing Office
Washington, DC 20402
Stock Number 001-000-04484-2

▶ **Booklet:** *Your Financial Plan*
Cost: $1.25
Contains: A very readable and informative introduction to financial planning. Includes worksheets.
From: Money Management Institute
Household Financial Services
2700 Sanders Road
Prospect Heights, IL 60070

When you complete your net-worth statements, you and your future spouse should review them thoroughly. Questioning your future spouse's financial honesty, however, may be unthinkable for you as your wedding date approaches. This is another reason why, for your own protection, you should retain your own attorney who can detect signs that assets or debts are being hidden.

4. Neither you nor your spouse may be coerced into signing a prenuptial agreement. In theory, your prenuptial agreement would be unenforceable if you told your future spouse, "I won't marry you unless you sign this agreement." In practice, however, the courts recognize that your desire to protect your assets or your dependent children from a previous marriage through a premarital agreement is a legitimate part of your decision to marry. A court would likely enforce a prenuptial agreement passing title to your home to your children even if it were proven that your spouse knew that accepting such a provision was critical to your decision to marry.

If your future spouse offered you $25,000 in cash or a new car in exchange for signing a prenuptial agreement, however, a court probably would consider that a form of coercion. Pressure from parents or other relatives to sign a prenuptial agreement also is considered coercion. For example:

- Your future father-in-law informs you that he will not allow the marriage unless you agree to give up all claims to your future spouse's share of the family business.
- Your fiancé tells you that his ex-wife will not let him see the children unless you give up all your claims to his assets.

Once again, the best way to eliminate both the appearance and the opportunity for coercion is to hire your own attorney to negotiate the prenuptial agreement.

PRENUPTIAL AGREEMENTS AND DIVORCE—A POTENTIAL MINEFIELD

The institution of marriage is considered so important to the stability of our society that courts will not enforce prenuptial agreements that:

- Are drawn up in contemplation of an eventual divorce
- Facilitate the process of obtaining a divorce

This means that neither partner can, in a prenuptial agreement, waive rights to contest a divorce action, be represented by an attorney in a divorce action, agree not to seek custody of the children, or give up any other legal rights or protections. Almost all prenuptial agreements state that the agreement is not being drawn up in contemplation of divorce.

Many state courts also strike down property settlements that may encourage divorce, either because they are too low or too high. For example:

- An agreement that gives one spouse half of the other's $250,000 net worth, even if the marriage ends in a year
- An agreement that provides one spouse with a property settlement of $1,000 for each year of marriage, even though the other spouse has a net worth of $250,000

The subject of alimony is even more difficult. Eleven states prohibit any agreement on the subject before marriage. In many other states, fixing alimony payments that will be enforced by the court requires consulting a complicated set of laws and judicial precedents.

These difficulties, however, do not mean that you should not draw up a prenuptial agreement if you or your spouse has significantly higher assets than the other. Indeed, numerous studies have shown that such prenuptial agreements are even more important in avoiding expensive and emotionally draining legal battles at the end of a marriage. What this does point out is the need for both partners to retain skilled legal help if one partner has significantly higher assets than the other partner. The courts want to make sure that marrying a wealthy person is not an easy way to get rich and that a wealthy person doesn't take advantage of a less-well-off spouse.

CAN A PRENUPTIAL AGREEMENT BE CHANGED OR CANCELED AFTER MARRIAGE?

Prenuptial agreements can be modified or canceled by written agreement during a marriage. State courts, however, examine such agreements, called marital agreements, with even greater scrutiny than they do prenuptial agreements. Even the slightest suggestion of possible coercion, concealment of assets, contemplation of divorce, or other discrepancies will likely void the marital agreement.

Marital agreements are growing in popularity. They are most useful when a significant change in circumstances has occurred since the prenuptial agreement was signed. For example, children from a previous marriage may have reached adulthood or may have become financially independent, the family home may have been sold, or your spouse may have decided that you should inherit his share of the family business rather than other relatives inheriting his share. In these cases, amending or overriding the prenuptial agreement will lessen confusion in the event of death or divorce.

Experts recommend, however, that you shouldn't wait until the marriage has taken place to deal with issues that can be settled in a prenuptial agreement.

2

Safeguarding Your Home and Other Important Financial Assets

KEY FACTS

- Marriage is a financial union in which the old rule of "what's yours is yours, what's mine is mine" no longer applies.
- State laws, not agreements between you and your spouse, largely determine what is marital property, what is separate property, what is joint debt, and what is separate debt.
- Court respect of marital privacy largely leaves decisions on how income should be spent to you and your spouse.
- The only way to protect yourself financially is to become actively involved in every aspect of managing your money.

For centuries, marriage has been a financial as well as a romantic union. Under English common law, which was the basis of American law as well, the husband had total legal control over all the couple's property, even property the wife had brought to the marriage. In return, the husband assumed total legal responsibility for supporting his wife and children.

This relationship began to change during the mid-1800s, when states passed laws giving married women the right to retain in their own name property they brought to their marriages. The final death knell was sounded in 1979 by the U.S. Supreme Court, which held in the case of *Orr v. Orr* that it is unconstitutional to impose primary support obligations on husbands and only secondary obligations on wives.

The result is that both spouses incur significant mutual financial rights and responsibilities. This is why experts recommend that couples work together to manage all their personal finances. Making intelligent decisions based on sound legal and financial knowledge protects both husband and wife from unpleasant shocks, even disaster, should the marriage end in death or divorce. This knowledge includes understanding the differences between marital property and separate property and the differences between family debt and separate debt. It also involves an understanding of who is responsible for supporting the family under what specific circumstances.

WHAT IS MARITAL PROPERTY?

Marital property refers to almost all types of property acquired by either spouse during a marriage. In the event of divorce, the court, not the two partners, divides the marital property in accordance with the laws of the state. Although state laws vary, marital property generally includes:

wages
stock options
interest
dividends
pensions
family business profits
household goods

business goodwill
bank accounts
motor vehicles
real estate
tax refunds
life insurance policies
collections
copyrights
patents

In many states, increases during marriage in the value of business, real estate, or investments owned before the marriage also are considered marital property, unless specifically exempted by a prenuptial agreement (see Chapter 1).

Who Controls Marital Property During the Marriage?

With one exception, American states view marital property in one of two major ways:

1. Community-property states. The following states define marital property as "community property":

Arizona
California
Idaho
Louisiana
Nevada
New Mexico
Texas
Washington
Wisconsin (follows a system similar to community property but does not use that term)

In these states, all marital property is considered joint property to which both partners have equal rights. For example, even though you purchase $10,000 in stock in your own name with your own earnings, your spouse has equal claim on and control over those funds. In community-property states, the courts generally divide all marital property equally between the two spouses upon divorce (for more details, see Chapter 8).

2. Equitable-distribution states. In every other state (except Mississippi) and the District of Columbia, each spouse has the right to hold property individually instead of jointly. For instance, if you purchase $10,000 in stock with money you earned, your spouse has no direct claim on or control over those funds during marriage. When a couple divorces, however, the courts have the right to distribute all marital property, including that held individually by either spouse, to achieve an "equitable" or "fair" settlement.

Mississippi is the only state that adheres to a system similar to the old English common law. In Mississippi, property during and after marriage is owned by the person whose name is on the title, regardless of contributions toward its purchase. For example, if the title to your home is in your spouse's name, your spouse retains ownership upon divorce, even if you contributed half the down payment and made half the mortgage payments.

WHAT IS SEPARATE PROPERTY?

Separate property is property that can be sold, given away, or otherwise disposed of without the consent of the other spouse. In the event of a divorce, separate property is not divided by the court but is retained by the spouse who owns it. Separate property generally includes:

- Any property owned before marriage
- Property purchased through the sale of property owned before marriage (e.g., a boat bought with the proceeds of the sale of stock)
- Pension benefits completely vested before marriage

- Property acquired through inheritance
- Property received as a gift given specifically to one spouse
- Property awarded to one spouse as a result of personal injury, negligence, malpractice, or similar legal action
- Property acquired after a legal separation
- Additional property defined as separate property in a legally valid prenuptial agreement

Can Separate Property Become Marital Property?

Separate property can become marital property in certain circumstances if it is "commingled" or joined with marital property in a way that the expenditures are untraceable. For example, you own a piece of property before you are married. After your marriage, you sell the property and deposit $5,000 of the proceeds in your joint checking account to be used to meet regular household expenses. Because the specific use of the money is hard or impossible to trace, it has become marital property.

If that $5,000 were used for a specific traceable purchase, however, such as the down payment for an automobile, it still would be considered separate property. In the event of a divorce, you would be entitled to a reimbursement of $5,000 before the remaining value of the car was distributed as part of the marital property.

WHO IS RESPONSIBLE FOR DEBTS INCURRED DURING MARRIAGE?

Fully understanding who is responsible for repaying debts is at least as important as understanding the difference between marital and separate property. Although state laws about debt vary more than laws concerning property ownership, all of the laws divide debts incurred during marriage into one of two types:

1. Joint or community debts. These are obligations for which *both* spouses are legally responsible. To satisfy the debts, creditors look:

- First, to the couple's jointly owned or community property
- Second, to the separate property of each partner

2. Separate debts. These are obligations for which only one spouse is legally responsible. To satisfy these debts, creditors look:

- First, to the separate property of the indebted spouse
- Second, to the jointly owned or community property of the couple

Creditors, however, may not look to the separate property of the other spouse.

What Is Joint Debt?

The obligations for which both husband and wife are jointly responsible differ in community-property states and equitable-distribution states.

1. Community-property states consider most debts incurred during marriage as community debts, with the following two exceptions:

- Debts for which the creditor looks only to the separate property of one spouse for payment. For example, you take out a second mortgage loan to pay for an addition on a vacation home that you owned before your marriage. This mortgage is not a community loan if the lender is looking only to the equity in that vacation home when agreeing to make the loan.
- Debts that do not benefit the "community"; that is, debts that may contribute to the breakup of the marriage. For example, you are not liable if your spouse charges a trip to Florida to meet a lover.

2. Equitable-distribution states generally consider the following types of debts as joint debts:

- Debts incurred in the name of both spouses or debts based on the assets and credit histories of both spouses. This category includes:
  - — Loans for property held jointly, such as a house or an automobile
  - — Bank-overdraft provisions and other credit lines tied to joint accounts
  - — Credit cards and charge accounts in the names of both spouses
- Debts incurred by one spouse with the knowledge or the permission of the other. For example, you may have given your spouse a credit card in his or her name on an account opened on the basis of your separate credit history. You are responsible for charges made on that card, even if you did not authorize the specific purchase. You also may be liable for charges made by your spouse on your credit card, if you previously allowed your spouse to use that card.
- Debts incurred for the necessities of life, including housing, food, clothing, and medical care. For instance, your spouse is equally liable with you for charges resulting from your admission to the hospital for medical treatment.

In equitable-distribution states, you are not personally liable for your spouse's debt if:

- The debt was incurred solely by your spouse. For example, your spouse obtains a credit card in his or her own name.
- The debt was not incurred for a family necessity. For instance, your spouse charges an expensive car stereo system for his or her own vehicle.

Creditors can look to your jointly owned property, however, such as your bank accounts or your house, to satisfy debts incurred separately by your spouse.

Between the debts that are clearly joint and those that are clearly separate are those debts that fall into a gray area in which obligations may vary widely from state to state and from court to court. For instance, your spouse uses a personal credit card to surprise you with a vacation to Bermuda. In some states, the credit-card company may be allowed to look to you to satisfy the debt because you benefited from the debt. In other states, you may not be legally liable to repay the debt, but the court may consider such a debt as part of the community debt in divorce proceedings.

Who Is Responsible for Debts Incurred Before Marriage?

You are responsible for debts that you incurred before your marriage, unless your spouse accepts partial or full responsibility through a prenuptial agreement. For example, you have a balance of $1,000 on a credit card when you marry. To satisfy this debt, the creditor looks first to your separate property, and then second, to your joint property, such as a joint bank account. Your spouse, however, may assume responsibility through a prenuptial agreement. This type of agreement is especially common when the spouse with the debts is quitting his or her own job to go back to school or to raise a family.

In some states, you may be liable to a degree for debts that your spouse incurred before marriage if he or she has transferred separate property to you. The purpose of these provisions is to prevent a person from escaping responsibility for legitimate debts by transferring assets to a spouse. Your liability in such cases, however, extends only to the value of the transferred property. For example, you may be liable for up to $5,000 of your spouse's premarital debts if he or she transfers stocks worth $5,000 to you.

WHO IS RESPONSIBLE FOR SUPPORTING YOUR FAMILY?

More than a decade ago, the U.S. Supreme Court struck down any remaining laws that made the husband solely responsible for supporting his family. Today, both spouses share the responsibility of providing for themselves and their children the necessities of life, such as food, shelter, clothing, and medical care.

How Do the Courts Define That Responsibility?

Even though laws mandating that the husband solely support the family have been struck down, courts in many states still consider the husband the primary provider. If the husband works, he is obligated to use his wages and other property to provide the necessities. If he has sufficient income but chooses not to use it to support his family, the wife can legally charge necessities to him.

The legal difference between today's law and the law of three decades ago is the responsibility of the wife in the event that her husband is unable to work or to find work, or in the event that his income is not sufficient. In these circumstances, the wife must legally use her income and assets to meet necessary family expenses. If she doesn't have a job, she must try to find one before the family can seek public assistance.

Who is responsible for providing the necessities if both spouses work? This situation, which is increasingly common today, represents a large gray area into which most courts are very reluctant to step unless the welfare of children is involved. For example, you and your spouse may earn similar salaries, but your spouse refuses to contribute a dime toward household expenses. Even though it may be unfair that household expenses take all of your earnings, the courts probably would not intervene. The courts, however, would likely force your spouse to contribute if you were unable to provide adequate housing or medical care for your children.

Who Is Responsible for Expenses Beyond the Necessities?

Because of the strongly established legal right to marital

privacy, courts will not become involved in the financial relationships of a couple if the necessities of life are being provided. To date, court rulings have required working spouses to provide only a very minimal standard of living. For example, in one famous case, an elderly Nebraska farm wife sued her wealthy husband because he provided only a primitive home with no indoor plumbing and only one new dress every five years. The court ruled that that level of support, although unfair, provided the necessities of life. The woman's only recourse to get a share of her husband's wealth was to file for divorce.

Standards in your state may not be quite so primitive. No court, however, will order your spouse, no matter how wealthy, to provide you with an automobile, vacations, jewelry, new furniture, stylish clothing, a bigger house, appliances, entertainment, dinners out, or any other expense that is not a matter of subsistence.

HOW TO PROTECT YOURSELF FINANCIALLY DURING MARRIAGE

The General Mills American Family Survey found that married couples are four times more likely to argue about money than about any other subject. Differences ranging from misunderstandings to outright deceptions are the cause of the most intense bitterness during divorce proceedings. Managing your marital finances prudently and openly not only will protect your assets in the event that your marriage should end but also will eliminate the source of much conflict while your marriage continues.

The steps you should take to protect yourself financially during marriage are:

1. Sign a prenuptial agreement dealing with all premarital assets and obligations. As emphasized in Chapter 1, such agreements are vital if either spouse brings significant property or debts to a marriage.

2. Keep your separate property separate. In all states, property you bring to a marriage and property you acquire through inheritance, gifts, injury claims, or certain other circumstances is not considered marital property. If kept separate, this property is not subject to disposition by the courts and is exempt from claims by your spouse's creditors.

If you do contribute some of your separate property toward the purchase of a jointly owned asset, as many couples do, you should maintain a written record of your contribution. For example, if you have records proving that you contributed $10,000 toward the purchase of your home, you will be reimbursed for that $10,000 before the remaining equity in the home is divided as marital property or as part of your spouse's estate.

If you must use separate property to meet household expenses, you should pay bills from your separate account rather than commingling the funds in your joint accounts.

3. Prepare and follow a household budget. Good communication about finances begins with a joint agreement on how your marital income should be allocated. A written budget makes it easier to:

- Prevent impulse spending
- Decide what you can and can't afford
- Increase dollars for savings
- Make decisions about major purchases
- Protect against problems and prepare for emergencies

Preparing a budget means adding up your total income and balancing it against your expenses. Your income may include:

wages and salaries
interest
dividends
proceeds from sales of assets
rents on property
profits from business
repayment of personal loans

Your expenses fall into one of two categories. Fixed expenses are those that you have to pay in specific amounts at specific times. Some, such as rent, mortgage payments, utility payments, and taxes, you pay monthly or they may be deducted from every paycheck. Others, such as insurance payments or car-registration fees, are payable quarterly or annually. A list of common fixed expenses includes:

rent
mortgage payments
maintenance fees
taxes
utilities
garbage pickup and other home services
installment payments on credit cards, car loans, etc.
insurance payments
transportation expenses
membership dues
contributions to churches and other charities
tuition and other educational expenses
subscriptions
savings and investments

Many other expenses are flexible, varying from week to week or month to month. These include:

food eaten at home
restaurant meals
clothing
laundry and dry cleaning
purchase of furniture and appliances
household maintenance and repair
home improvements
household supplies
household help
gifts
vacations
health expenses (not covered by insurance)
personal care

entertainment
recreation
miscellaneous, such as stamps, tobacco, etc.

4. Establish and maintain a financial records filing system. The best way to adhere to a budget and guard against any unpleasant financial surprises is to create a well-organized financial filing system that allows you to find and inspect all your important records at any time. Even if you are not the one who pays the bills, you should take the time to periodically review bank statements, statements from mutual funds and brokerage firms, credit-card and loan bills, insurance policy summaries, and other documents.

To set up a system, experts recommend you create the following file folders:

- **Banking:** Monthly statements, canceled checks, deposit slips, and a list of all accounts
- **Credit:** All credit agreements, charge slips, and monthly statements
- **Employment and business expenses:** Pay stubs, information on employee benefits, copies of expense reports, and any other business-related records
- **Contributions:** Receipts, correspondence, logbook of the expenses you incur as a volunteer, and all other records relating to charitable contributions
- **Pension plans and IRAs:** All documents related to your retirement accounts
- **Insurance:** Copies of policies, invoices, claims, and a copy of your home inventory
- **Investments:** All records related to stocks, bonds, mutual funds, and other investments
- **Medical and dental:** List of doctors and other medical professionals you have consulted, a copy of medical records, bills, inoculation records, and health-insurance claims
- **Residence:** Copies of leases, rent checks, copies of mortgage papers, mortgage statements, home-maintenance receipts, home-improvement records, utility records, and any other records connected with your home

- **Investment real estate:** Records related to any other real estate you own
- **Receipts and warranties:** Receipts and warranties that don't fit into other categories
- **Taxes:** Copies of all returns and other associated information
- **Personal:** Photocopies of important papers, list of safe-deposit boxes, inventory of collections, membership cards in organizations, and any other personal papers
- **Estate file:** See Chapter 5

Several tools can be used to help you organize your personal finances. One recommendation is:

▶ **Book:** *Dollar Watch: The Personal Financial Organizer*
Cost: $19.95 plus $3.00 postage and handling
Contains: A complete and easy-to-use financial planner
From: Datamax
132 Nassau Street
New York, NY 10038

---

5. Jointly participate in assembling tax records, preparing returns, and developing tax-reduction strategies. A married couple's right to file joint income tax returns brings with it both advantages and responsibilities that both spouses should understand. This subject is covered in depth in Chapter 3.

6. Jointly participate in retirement planning. Planning for retirement, including protecting your rights to Social Security and pension benefits, must begin the day either you or your spouse begin to work. This subject is examined thoroughly in Chapter 4.

7. Jointly participate in estate planning, including the drafting of a will. Estate planning is an extremely important and comprehensive subject that must be considered when all financial decisions are made, such as exactly how you and your spouse will hold title to property. Chapter 5 covers this subject in depth.

3

Understanding Your Tax Benefits and Liabilities

KEY FACTS

- Your tax status changes when you marry. You and your spouse must understand all the implications of this change.
- Legal separation presents you and your spouse with a number of tax options that must be dealt with in a separation agreement.
- The structure of a divorce settlement has major tax consequences.

Few of us like to spend time thinking about income taxes, especially when we're caught up in the joy and excitement of planning an upcoming marriage. But beginning and ending a marriage legally changes your tax status and your tax obligations. To protect yourself legally and financially, you should understand the benefits and liabilities of each tax-filing status, obtain as much information about taxes as you can, find the most competent tax-preparation assistance, and take tax consequences into consideration when you separate or divorce.

WHAT ARE THE DEFINITIONS OF EACH TAX-FILING STATUS?

When filing your federal income tax return, you must select one tax-filing status from the five mandated by law. Although there are only three federal tax rates (15, 28, and 33 percent), the income level at which rates increase is different for each tax status. Deductions, credits, and benefits also vary for each status. The five tax statuses are:

1. Single. You may choose the single status if you were:

- Unmarried during the year
- Divorced during the year
- Legally separated during the year

Single filers pay higher tax rates on a larger percentage of their incomes than filers in any other status except in the married, filing separately status.

2. Married, filing jointly. You may claim this status if you are married and if you and your spouse agree to file a joint return. You also would be considered married for the whole year if:

- You and your spouse were living apart but were not divorced.
- You and your spouse were separated by an interlocutory, not final, decree of divorce.
- Your spouse died during the year but you did not remarry.

Married couples filing jointly pay the lowest rates of any filing status. Because of the limits on deductions and tax credits, however, a married couple may pay more taxes on their combined incomes than they would have paid if each spouse were single. This is called the "marriage penalty."

3. Married, filing separately. You may claim this status if you were considered married for the entire year under any of the previously mentioned criteria. If your spouse does not agree to file a joint return, you must choose this status. Married people filing separately pay higher tax rates on a higher percentage of their income than any other tax filers.

4. Head of household. You can choose this status if you meet both of the following criteria:

- You were unmarried during the year or were considered unmarried because you were divorced or legally separated during the year.
- You paid more than half the costs of maintaining a home for you and at least one of the following dependents:

child
parent
grandparent
brother or sister
stepbrother or stepsister
stepparent
mother-in-law or father-in-law
brother-in-law or sister-in-law
son-in-law or daughter-in-law
aunt or uncle if related by blood
niece or nephew if related by blood

A head of household pays a lower tax rate than a person who files as either single or married, filing separately.

5. Qualified widow or widower. You may elect to choose this status for the two calendar years following the year in which your spouse died if:

- You have not remarried.
- You paid for more than half the cost of maintaining a home for a dependent child, stepchild, adopted child, or foster child.

As a qualified widow or widower, you are entitled to the same low tax rates and high standard deduction as that of a couple who are married and filing jointly.

For more information, you can obtain the following federal tax publications that are free and will be mailed to your home (within seven to ten working days) if you call tollfree: (800) 424-3676:

Pub. 17: *Your Federal Income Tax*
An extensive line-by-line explanation of the items on Form 1040, as well as Schedules A, B, D, E, R, and SE, and Forms W-2, 2106, 2119, 2441, and 3903. Includes examples of typical situations and sample filled-in forms.

Pub. 501: *Exemptions and Standard Deduction*
Explains how and when you can take exemptions for yourself and dependents and provides the higher standard-deduction amounts for age and blindness.

Pub. 502: *Medical and Dental Expenses*
Explains how medical and dental expenses may be deducted and includes many tips on deductions that you may overlook.

Pub. 554: *Tax Information for Older Americans*
Focuses on tax information and deductions specially applicable to older Americans. Includes many examples and filled-in forms.

Pub. 555: *Community Property and the Federal Income Tax*
Provides information on special tax problems and situations for married, separated, and divorced couples in community-property states.

Pub. 448: *Federal Estate and Gift Taxes*
Explains in detail the federal estate taxes and the regulations on taxing gifts.

Pub. 504: *Tax Information for Divorced and Separated Individuals*

Explains the tax rules on filing status and claiming dependents and discusses the tax treatment of alimony and property settlements.

Pub. 524: *Credit for the Elderly or for the Permanently and Totally Disabled*
Explains how to figure the credit for those age 65 and older, as well as how to calculate the credit for the disabled.

Pub. 529: *Miscellaneous Deductions*
Explains such deductions as employee expenses, union dues, business education expenses, and other deductions that fall into the miscellaneous category on Schedule A.

Pub. 530: *Tax Information for Owners of Homes, Condominiums, and Cooperative Apartments*
Explains in detail the deductions available for these types of property owners.

Pub. 545: *Interest Expense*
Explains what interest expenses can and cannot be deducted.

Pub. 550: *Investment Income and Expenses*
Explains the tax treatment of income received from all types of investments.

Pub. 552: *Record Keeping for Individuals and a List of Tax Publications*
Helps taxpayers decide what records to keep and how to organize their tax information.

Pub. 559: *Tax Information for Survivors, Executors, and Administrators*
Covers the many questions that arise from the death of a spouse, relative, or other loved one.

Pub. 575: *Pension and Annuity Income*
Explains how to report income from pensions and

annuities and discusses the rules for handling lump-sum distributions from profit-sharing or pension plans.

Pub. 590: *Individual Retirement Arrangements*
Explains the benefits of Individual Retirement Accounts (IRAs) and the tax treatments of such investments.

Pub. 907: *Tax Information for Handicapped and Disabled Individuals*
Explains the tax rules for those who are handicapped or disabled, or for those who have handicapped or disabled dependents.

Pub. 915: *Social Security Benefits and Equivalent Railroad Retirement Benefits*
Provides tax information for recipients of Social Security and Railroad Retirement benefits.

Pub. 929: *Tax Rules for Children and Dependents*
Explains the new tax laws affecting children and other dependents.

DOES THE TIMING OF YOUR WEDDING HAVE TAX CONSEQUENCES?

If you are planning a wedding at the end of a year, the timing of your wedding can increase or decrease the total taxes that you and your spouse will have to pay. As a general rule, if both you and your spouse work and make significant incomes, you would pay higher taxes if you were married, filing jointly, than if you were single. In this case, you would save money by marrying in January rather than in December.

If one of you has little or no income, you would pay less money if you were married, filing jointly, than if you were single. In this situation, you would save money by marrying in December rather than in January.

HOW CAN YOU MINIMIZE YOUR JOINT TAX LIABILITY WHILE YOU ARE MARRIED?

Thoroughly understanding the tax system is the foundation for saving money on your taxes. You also can minimize your liability by carefully considering the following suggestions.

Choose the Right Tax-Filing Status

Most married couples will pay less taxes if they file jointly rather than if they file separately because of the substantial difference in tax rates. You should understand, however, that filing jointly makes both spouses equally liable for interest, penalties, and other consequences of filing an inaccurate, incomplete, late, or fraudulent tax return. You should not agree to file a joint return with your spouse if you suspect that he or she is being dishonest or irresponsible about personal finances and tax preparation. Remember, you have no legal obligation to file jointly if you are married.

Even if you trust your spouse, you may be better off filing separately in certain circumstances, including:

- One of you had high medical expenses during the year. Because medical expenses are deductible only over 7.5 percent of your adjusted gross income, your additional deduction may make filing separately worthwhile.
- One of you had substantial unreimbursed employee business expenses during the year. Again, the deduction for these expenses is related to your total income.
- One of you had other write-offs, such as capital losses or casualty losses, that would be more beneficial to include on a separate return.

If you have any doubts about which filing status to select, you should compute your tax liability under both options.

Group Deductions into One Tax Year

Certain expenses, such as mortgage-interest payments and charitable contributions, are deductible only if your total deductions exceed the standard deduction in any one year. Other deductions must meet the additional requirement of exceeding a certain percentage of your income. In both cases, you may be able to benefit and not lose deductions by grouping expenses into one year.

For example, you may want to schedule elective surgery, dental work, or other medical procedures at the end of a year in which your medical expenses have been high, rather than waiting until January or February. Or you may schedule your family's yearly physicals in early January and late December of one year to maximize the deductions.

Many couples also save money by making charitable contributions every other year or every third year. Certain unreimbursed employee business expenses also can be grouped.

Take Advantage of Tax-Deferred Retirement Accounts

You should consult the retirement planning and pension section in Chapter 4 for more information about the considerable tax advantages of both individual and certain employer pension arrangements.

Obtain Information About the Tax Consequences of Major Financial Decisions and Purchases

Chapter 5 discusses in detail the necessity of seeking professional advice about the estate-planning implications of all the major financial decisions and purchases that you make. At the same time, you should ask the financial professional for information about minimizing the tax consequences.

Obtain the Best Professional Help When Preparing Your Tax Returns

Unless your tax returns are very simple or unless you or your spouse are extremely knowledgeable about your federal and state income tax regulations, you probably will save money by having your taxes professionally prepared. Among your tax-preparation options are:

1. National tax services. By far the largest of these services is H&R Block, which annually opens temporary offices in thousands of storefronts across the country. Tax preparers hired by Block are required to attend a 75-hour training course in tax preparation, and other national services require similar training. The advantages of these services are:

- They are inexpensive, with the average fee ranging from $30 to $100.
- Block and several other companies guarantee their work, paying any penalties assessed because of their mistakes.
- A representative will accompany a customer to an audit to explain how the return was computed.

The disadvantages of these services include:

- The preparers are not qualified to handle complicated returns.
- While these preparers can appear to explain mathematical calculations, they cannot represent you before the Internal Revenue Service (IRS).
- While the service may promise to pay any penalties and interest incurred, you are responsible for additional taxes levied by the IRS should the preparer make a mistake.
- They provide no tax-planning advice.

2. Local tax services. Locally owned and operated tax-preparation services spring up every tax season in many localities. Their advantages are:

- They are very inexpensive.
- Some preparers have extensive knowledge of state and local taxes.
- Some guarantee to pay any penalties and interest caused by their errors.

The disadvantages of dealing with local services are:

- Many preparers have little or no training.
- Some are fly-by-night operators who disappear after April 15th, leaving you unable to answer IRS inquiries about your return.
- Some may fail to actually file your returns, leaving you liable for severe penalties.
- Most are not qualified to handle complicated returns.
- These preparers cannot represent you before the IRS.
- They provide no tax-planning information.

3. Enrolled agents. An enrolled agent has demonstrated special competence in the field of taxation and has been authorized to represent taxpayers before all administrative levels of the IRS. To become an enrolled agent, a person must pass a comprehensive two-day examination given by the U.S. Treasury Department or must have at least five years' service as an employee of the IRS. Enrolled agents also must meet ethical standards.

The advantages of enlisting an enrolled agent to prepare your return are:

- The agent's fees generally are lower than those of certified public accountants (CPAs) and tax attorneys.
- The agent is a full-time tax specialist.
- The agent must keep up with changes in tax laws through continuing education, or the agent may lose IRS certification.
- The agent can represent you through all stages of an audit or an appeal process with the IRS.
- The agent offers tax-planning advice.

The disadvantages of employing an enrolled agent are:

- The agent is not as qualified to help you with overall financial planning as a CPA is.
- Unlike a tax attorney, the agent cannot represent you in federal courts.

For more information about enrolled agents and for referral to one or more in your area, contact:

▶ **Organization:** National Association of Enrolled Agents
Cost of referral: Free
From: National Association of Enrolled Agents
6000 Executive Boulevard, Suite 205
Rockville, MD 20852
(800) 424-4339 (24-hour service)

---

4. Public accountants. Public accountants normally have academic degrees in accounting and, in many states, are licensed by the state. About 40 percent of the members of the National Society of Public Accountants have met the requirements to become enrolled agents, and these accountants are most likely to provide competent tax preparation and counseling.

5. Certified public accountants. Certified public accountants (CPAs) must have degrees in accounting, must have passed a rigorous national exam, must be licensed by their states, and must meet continuing-education requirements. The advantages of hiring CPAs are:

- They are highly trained and regulated by state and industry associations.
- They are the most qualified professionals to provide year-round financial and tax-planning advice.
- They are allowed to represent you before the IRS.

The disadvantages of hiring CPAs are:

- Their fees range from $100 an hour and upward.
- Not all CPAs are tax experts.
- Some CPAs handle only business returns, not individual returns.

To find a CPA in your area, contact:

▶ **Organization:** American Institute of CPAs
1211 Avenue of the Americas
New York, NY 10036
(212) 575-6200

---

6. Tax attorneys. Tax attorneys are specialists in tax law. Tax attorneys seldom prepare individual returns. Rather, they provide legal advice in complicated matters involving taxes, investments, and estate planning. Their fees can range from $100 to $400 an hour. Tax attorneys are the only professionals allowed to represent you in criminal cases or in other tax appeals that reach the courts.

To find a tax attorney, look in your telephone directory under "Lawyer Referral Service" or "Attorney Referral Service."

HOW DOES YOUR TAX STATUS CHANGE WHEN YOU ARE SEPARATED?

Couples who separate informally or under the terms of a written agreement still are considered married and must choose between filing jointly or separately as married individuals. Because filing jointly is much more advantageous in most cases, most separation agreements call for joint filing. For your protection, however, you should have your attorney include a clause making your spouse indemnify you against any liability resulting from his or her unstated income or overstated deductions.

If you and your spouse separate under a written agreement and if you have custody of a child for more than half a year, you may be eligible to file as a head of household. Your spouse then would be forced to file under the much less preferable married, filing separately status. For this reason, your attorney may be able to negotiate higher temporary support payments or other advantageous terms in exchange for your agreement to file jointly.

If you and your spouse have separated under a court decree, or judicial separation (see Chapter 8), you are considered unmarried and may elect to file as single or, if you are eligible, as head of household. If both you and your spouse work, you may pay lower taxes filing separately than if you file jointly as a married couple.

WHAT ARE THE POTENTIAL TAX BENEFITS AND LIABILITIES OF DIVORCE?

Professional tax advice is required when negotiating a divorce settlement. Among the issues that have tax consequences are:

1. Child support. Child-support payments are not tax-deductible for the spouse who pays and they are not taxable income for the spouse who receives the payments. Under present law, the parent with custody automatically is entitled to the tax exemption for that child, unless the custodial parent releases the claim to the exemption by filing IRS Form 8332. Because this tax exemption is worth more to the parent with the higher income, many divorce settlements are structured so that the parent paying child support contributes a higher amount in exchange for the exemption.

2. Alimony. Alimony payments, within certain maximum-dollar amounts, are tax-deductible for the payer and taxable to the recipient. In some cases, certain benefits provided to one spouse, such as payment of life-insurance premiums or mortgages, may be deductible as alimony.

The amount of total support payments that is considered alimony is a critical issue in settlement negotiations. For example, you may agree to increase the portion of your support attributed to alimony and decrease the amount attributed to child support in exchange for a higher overall support figure or a larger property settlement. The IRS, however, may disallow deduction of alimony that really is child support in disguise—for example, alimony that ceases within six months of a child reaching adulthood.

3. Property settlement. All property transferred between married couples or between divorced couples as part of a divorce decree is exempt from taxation. Such transfers, however, can have tax consequences in the future for both parties.

For example, the spouse receiving the property must pay any capital-gains taxes on the entire appreciation when the property is sold. If, for instance, you and your spouse purchased a home for $50,000 that was worth $100,000 when it was transferred to you and you sold it five years later for $125,000, you must pay taxes on the full $75,000 appreciation, not just on the $25,000 appreciation that occurred since it was transferred to you. While you could avoid paying taxes by rolling over the profit by investing it in another home, you still would have to pay taxes on the sale of stocks, bonds, mutual-fund shares, artwork, a vacation home, or other property.

Giving up the right to live in a home can have tax consequences, too. For example, many divorce settlements require that the family home be sold after a period of years, with the proceeds split between the spouse who lived in the home and the spouse who moved out. If that period is more than 18 months, the spouse who moved out must pay tax on the capital gains, because the home was no longer his or her principal residence.

As a result, all tax consequences enter into the divorce

negotiations. For instance, one spouse may agree to allow the other spouse to increase tax deductions by transferring some property over a period of time as alimony, in exchange for a larger overall settlement. To protect yourself, you never should agree to such provisions without seeking professional counsel and without thoroughly understanding the consequences.

4

Protect Your Social Security, Pensions, and Other Retirement Benefits

KEY FACTS

- Social Security is an invaluable package of benefits. You may lose some or all of these benefits, however, if you fail to protect your rights.
- Your eligibility for coverage under Medicare directly depends on your eligibility for Social Security benefits.
- Despite new protections under federal law, only 3 percent of surviving widows in the United States are receiving benefit checks from their husbands' pensions.
- Taking advantage of all of your rights to open tax-deferred retirement accounts can substantially increase your standard of living when you stop working.

Safeguarding your rights to Social Security, pensions, Medicare, and retirement funds never has been more important. One reason is that modern medicine has produced such a significant increase in longevity that the average person who retires has nearly one-quarter of his or her life to look forward to. Having a sufficient income to meet expenses, especially medical costs, can make these years the most enjoyable years of your life.

A second reason is that you begin paying for Social Security, Medicare, and pensions from the time you begin to work. It is vital that you are properly credited with these contributions and that you retain all your rights to pension and retirement funds that are yours alone or are part of your marital property.

Finally, the Social Security system provides important disability and survivor benefits that you, your spouse, and your children may have to rely on well before the retirement years.

HOW TO PROTECT YOUR RIGHTS TO SOCIAL SECURITY BENEFITS

The key to protecting your rights to Social Security benefits is by fully understanding the Social Security system.

What Is Social Security?

More than 38 million Americans, including 98 percent of those who are retired, currently receive monthly Social Security checks. If you are working or have worked, Social Security basically provides you with three types of benefits:

1. Retirement benefits for you, as well as for your spouse and dependent children
2. Disability benefits if you or your spouse are unable to work, as well as benefits for dependent children
3. Survivor's benefits after your death or the death of your spouse for minor children, disabled older children, and dependent elderly parents

How Are Social Security Benefits Earned?

Social Security benefits are based directly on earnings from employment and self-employment. You can qualify for benefits in one of three ways:

- Based on your own lifetime employment record
- Based on your spouse's employment record, if you are married
- Based on your ex-spouse's employment record, if your marriage lasted ten years *and* if you have not remarried

Eligibility for Social Security is measured in "work credits." You can earn a work credit by earning a certain amount of money during a calendar year, up to a maximum of four work credits. If you worked in 1990, you received one work credit for every $520 (gross income) you earned. If you earned $2,080 in 1990, you received the maximum four credits.

The number of work credits necessary to qualify for benefits depends on the type of benefits:

- To be eligible for retirement benefits, you must have earned 40 work credits. Once you have earned 40 work credits, you are permanently eligible, even if you never work again.
- To be eligible for disability benefits, you must have earned a minimum number of credits that increases with your age, e.g., 20 credits if you are age 31. You also must have earned a certain number of credits in a certain period of time before your disability.
- To be eligible for survivor benefits for your spouse and children, you also must have earned a minimum number of credits that increases with your age.

While eligibility for Social Security depends on the number of work credits you earn, the amount of the benefit checks that you, your spouse, or your dependent children would receive depends on the amount of Social Security tax that you paid over the course of your working career. For example, a worker who retired in 1990 would have received a check ranging from $465 to $965 per month, depending on his or her earnings over a lifetime.

If you qualify to receive retirement benefits on the basis of your spouse's or ex-spouse's earnings record, you can choose between receiving 50 percent of your spouse's or ex-spouse's benefit or benefits based on your own earnings record.

How Can I Find Out How Many Credits I've Earned and What My Benefits Are Likely to Be?

Both you and your spouse can obtain a statement from the Social Security Administration that contains:

- A year-by-year record of the work credits you have earned and the amount of Social Security tax you have paid
- An estimate of the retirement benefits you would receive on retirement should your earnings level remain steady
- An estimate of the disability and survivor benefits you have earned

To receive this statement, you must submit Form SSA-7004, "Request for Earnings and Benefit Estimate Statement." A copy of this form, along with detailed information on every aspect of Social Security and pensions, is included in:

▶ **Book:** *Protect Your Social Security, Medicare, and Pension Benefits* by Tom and Nancy Biracree (Contemporary Books, 1991)
Cost: $7.95
From: Your local bookstore.

You also can obtain copies of the form by calling the

tollfree Social Security Teleservice [(800) 234-5772] or by mail from the Consumer Information Center, PO Box 100, Pueblo, CO 81002.

When you receive your earnings and benefit statement, you should carefully check the information against your tax returns to be sure that your earnings were fully and properly recorded. In 1990, the Social Security Administration held almost $100 billion dollars in Social Security taxes that it was unable to credit to the proper account. A study by the U.S. House of Representatives indicated that at least another $100 billion in Social Security taxes were either improperly credited or never reported by employers. If you or your spouse find any errors, you should contact the Social Security Administration immediately by following the instructions on the earnings and benefit statement.

How to Protect Your Rights to Social Security Benefits

Verifying that all past earnings of you and your spouse have been accurately recorded is one important way to protect your right to receive benefits. Among the other steps you should take are:

1. Educate yourself about Social Security. One excellent way is to obtain a copy of the previously mentioned book, *Protect Your Social Security, Medicare, and Pension Benefits*. You also should obtain:

▶ **Pamphlets:** *An Introduction to Social Security, Social Security . . . How It Works for You, A Woman's Guide to Social Security*
Cost: Free
From: Social Security Teleservice
(800) 234-5772

▶ **Booklet:** *The Social Security Book: What Every Woman Absolutely Needs to Know* (D14117)
Cost: Free
From: AARP Fulfillment
1909 K Street, NW
Washington, DC 20049

2. Contact the Social Security Administration as soon as possible after your marriage if you have changed your name. If you don't, your future earnings may not be credited properly.

3. Make every possible effort to qualify for Social Security benefits on your own earnings record. The only way to absolutely guarantee that you will receive retirement benefits is to earn 40 work credits on your own. If you worked before you were married, you probably have a substantial start toward that goal. The level of earned income necessary to receive one work credit is so low that you could reach it by working just three hours per week at the minimum wage.

4. Submit a Form SSA-7004, "Request for Earnings and Benefit Estimate Statement," every three years and make sure your spouse does the same. Errors are much easier to spot and correct if they are caught early.

HOW TO PROTECT YOUR RIGHTS TO MEDICARE

Medicare is a federal health-insurance program for people age 65 and older, as well as certain people under age 65 who have been collecting Social Security disability benefits for 24 months. The hospital expenses covered under Medicare are paid by the Social Security taxes paid by you, other workers, and employers. The medical expenses covered under Medicare are paid from the general revenues of the U.S. government and from monthly premiums paid by those enrolled.

You automatically are entitled to Medicare coverage if you are receiving or are entitled to receive:

- Social Security benefits
- Railroad Retirement benefits
- Federal government pensions

If you haven't earned enough work credits to be eligible for Social Security benefits or if you are not eligible based on the earnings record of your present or ex-spouse, you still can enroll in Medicare—but you have to pay for the coverage out of your own pocket. In 1990, this cost was $175 per month. Eligibility for free Medicare hospital insurance is yet another reason why it is so important to protect your rights to Social Security benefits.

HOW TO PROTECT YOUR RIGHTS TO PENSION BENEFITS

A pension is any plan, fund, or program established by an employer, group of employers, or union that provides retirement income to employees or results in a deferral of income by employees until they leave their jobs or later. An employer is under no legal obligation to provide a pension plan. In fact, in 1990, 76.1 million Americans (46 percent of American workers) were covered by 870,000 pension plans. If you are one of them, you probably count on pension benefits as a crucial part of your retirement income.

Unfortunately, Congressional studies project that one-third of those 76.1 million workers will never receive one dime from the pension plan under which they are currently working. Millions of other workers will receive only part of the money they counted on. And surviving spouses of retired pension recipients fare the worst—only 3 percent of older American women are collecting monthly checks from their deceased husbands' pensions.

Who Is Eligible to Participate in a Pension Plan?

No company has to offer a pension plan. If your company offers a plan, however, federal law requires that all employees age 21 and older are eligible to participate in the plan after two years of employment. Participation cannot be denied on the basis of age.

What Are the Two Kinds of Pension Plans?

Your pension plan or your spouse's pension plan will be one of two types:

- **Defined benefit plans** are funded entirely by employer contributions and, upon an employee's retirement, pay a fixed benefit computed by a formula based on wages and years of service. Depending on when your plan began, your right to receive a pension becomes permanent, or "vested," after a period of time ranging from five to fifteen years. If your rights are vested, you will receive benefits at retirement age even if you leave the company. Defined benefit pension plans, up to certain limits, are guaranteed by an agency of the federal government in case the company dissolves the plan or files for bankruptcy.
- **Defined contribution plans** are funded by contributions from the employer based on a formula that often is determined by a company's profits. Under such plans, employees are frequently allowed to add contributions from their wages that are tax deferred. The benefits received on retirement depend on the rate of return received from investing the funds in each individual's pension account. All employee contributions are immediately vested when made, and employer contributions become vested after a period of employment that ranges from five to fifteen years. The balance in your pension account normally is given to you in a lump sum when you leave the company. Defined contribution plans, however, are not federally guaranteed.

How to Protect Your Rights to Your Own Pension

Despite a widespread increase in pension-fund abuses, the U.S. Department of Labor is able to audit only less than 1 percent of the nation's 870,000 pension plans each year. If you want your money to be available when you retire, you should:

1. Educate yourself on the subject of pensions. You definitely should obtain the following resources:

▶ **Book:** *Protect Your Social Security, Medicare, and Pension Benefits* by Tom and Nancy Biracree
Cost: $7.95
From: Your local bookstore

▶ **Booklets:** *What You Should Know About the Pension Law*
Often-Asked Questions About Employee Retirement Benefits
Cost: Free
From: Office of Public Affairs
Pension and Welfare Benefits Administration
U.S. Department of Labor
200 Constitution Avenue, NW
Washington, DC 20210

▶ **Booklet:** *Your Pension: Things You Should Know About Your Pension Plan*
Cost: Free
From: Pension Benefit Guaranty Corporation
2020 K Street, NW
Washington, DC 20006

▶ **Booklet:** *A Guide to Understanding Your Pension Plan*
Cost: Free
From: AARP
1909 K Street, NW
Washington, DC 20049

---

2. Educate yourself about your pension plan. According to federal law, you must receive a document called a "Summary Plan Description" when you become eligible for your company's pension plan. This document contains complete information about your plan, including a description of how benefits are calculated. If you did not automatically receive a copy, you should contact your company pension plan administrator. If you still are unable to get a copy, contact:

▶ **Organization:** Department of Labor
Public Disclosure Room
Room N-5707
200 Constitution Avenue, NW
Washington, DC 20210
(202) 523-8771
Fee: $ .10 per page for copies

---

3. Verify that the proper contributions are being made to your plan. On written request, your company pension plan administrator must annually furnish you with an "Individual Benefits Statement" that states the number of years you have been a participant in the plan, the benefits you have earned, the percentage of those benefits that is vested, the date on which your benefits will become completely vested, and, if you have a defined contributions plan, your account balance and a statement of how that balance has been invested.

You should take time to make sure all the information is accurate. If you are unable to obtain a statement, contact the Department of Labor at the address previously mentioned.

4. If you leave a job after your pension has become vested, make sure that you promptly notify the plan administrator every time your address changes. If your former company cannot locate you, you may not receive notifications of plan changes and terminations that could result in a loss of some or all of your benefits.

How to Protect Your Rights to Your Spouse's Pension After Divorce

A number of studies have shown that pension benefits are the largest or second largest marital asset in more than 75 percent of all divorces. Until recently, however, the courts had no statutory right to award part of the accrued pension sums or benefits. Fortunately, that problem was corrected in 1984 when Congress passed the Retirement Equity Act. Under the terms of that legislation, courts now have the authority to divide the balance in a pension account or the accrued benefits between an employee and a spouse on the termination of a marriage, just as the court has had the authority to divide other marital property. In other words, the pension benefits accrued by your spouse during marriage now are legally part of the marital property that you and your spouse will divide through an agreement between the two of you or as a result of decisions by a judge.

To receive your benefits from such a division, you must obtain from the court a document called a "Qualified Domestic Relations Order" (QDRO). You may receive the QDRO as part of a judicial separation or a divorce decree (see Chapter 8). Federal law mandates that a pension-plan trustee must comply with the terms of a valid QDRO.

How to Protect Your Rights to Your Spouse's Pension After His or Her Death

According to federal law, every company that offers a pension plan must offer a "joint-survivor benefit." That is, the company must offer a plan that provides for payments to a surviving spouse after the death of the worker receiving the pension. Although the joint-survivor payments are lower than those that end on the recipient's death (because payments will continue for additional years), this protection often may mean the difference between financial survival and extreme hardship.

Furthermore, as of 1985, federal law mandated that a

worker could not waive the right to receive a joint-survivor benefit without the signature of the spouse. That requirement sometimes is ignored. Some workers anxious to receive the highest immediate pension payment put pressure on a spouse to waive the right to a lower joint benefit or even forge a spouse's signature. In other instances, companies deliberately attempt to evade the law by illegally stopping payments on the worker's death.

To protect yourself from financial trouble in the retirement years, you should send for the following information:

▶ **Booklet:** *Protect Yourself: A Woman's Guide to Pension Rights* (D122J8)
Cost: Free
From: AARP
1909 K Street, NW
Washington, DC 20049

▶ **Booklet:** *Facts About the Joint and Survivor Benefits for the Retirement Equity Act*
Cost: Free
From: Office of Public Affairs
Pension and Welfare Benefits Administration
U.S. Department of Labor
200 Constitution Avenue, NW
Washington, DC 20210

PROTECT YOURSELF BY CONTRIBUTING TO AN INDIVIDUAL RETIREMENT ACCOUNT OR HAVING YOUR SPOUSE MAINTAIN A LIFE INSURANCE POLICY

Even if you don't work, you and your spouse can contribute up to $2,250 per year to an Individual Retirement Account, and up to $2,000 of that amount can be in your name. Even modest contributions over the years that accrue tax-free interest can provide retirement income that prevents financial hardship.

A second valuable asset can be a life insurance policy. Many workers drop life insurance coverage when their children are grown. Life insurance policies that have cash values, however, can be kept in effect until retirement at virtually no cost to the policy holder after the first few years. If your spouse's pension plan provides poor survivor benefits, you should explore the purchase of life insurance with a reputable agent.

5

Estate Planning and Preparation of a Will

KEY FACTS

- Estate planning is a vital financial activity for every married couple.
- Estate considerations should be taken into account when making every major financial transaction or decision, such as buying a home, opening a retirement account, having a child, making investments, or receiving an inheritance or other financial windfall.
- Next to a marriage license, a valid, up-to-date will is a married couple's most important legal document. Without a will, a spouse would inherit only one-third to one-half of the other spouse's estate.

Many couples don't spend any time on estate planning, for a variety of reasons. Some equate estate planning with "putting one's affairs in order," something that can be put off until "old age." Some find the subject of death uncomfortable or unpleasant. Still others believe that estate planning is important only for the wealthy. As a result, a majority of couples are financially unprepared for the death of one or both spouses. This lack of preparation often produces serious, even disastrous consequences at a time when the surviving spouse and children are emotionally devastated.

Estate planning should be a vital activity for every couple at every stage of their lives, not just in the retirement years. According to the U.S. Census Bureau, nine out of ten women will become widows. Nearly one-third of these women will be widows before they themselves turn 40, and the average age at which a woman becomes a widow is 53. In addition, 15 percent of all men become widowers, including the fathers of two million children under the age of eighteen.

To protect yourself and your children, you and your spouse should take action:

- To ensure that your heirs inherit the property you intend for them to inherit
- To provide that an estate is settled with a minimum of legal expense and delay
- To minimize or eliminate the reduction of an estate through taxation
- To appoint a guardian for dependent children (in the event of the death of both parents or of a single parent)

WHAT IS AN ESTATE?

Your estate consists of separate property and your share of marital property. Included are valuable property such as your home or investments as well as property with strictly sentimental value, such as photograph albums or letters. Your estate also includes any obligations, such as debts and unpaid taxes.

When you die, control over your estate is temporarily assumed by a special court, which in many states is called a probate court or a surrogate court. The court supervises the determination of your assets and liabilities and the payment of your debts and any taxes due. After subtracting fees for lawyers, accountants, and assessors, court costs, and other expenses, the court distributes the remaining property in one of two ways:

- **If you had executed a will,** your property would be distributed according to your wishes, as long as they weren't illegal or impossible to fulfill.
- **If you had no will** (or, in legal terms, died "intestate"), the court would distribute your property in a manner determined by the laws of your state. These laws provide that one-third to one-half of the property go to a surviving spouse. The remainder would be distributed to surviving children or, if there are no children, other immediate family members. If there is no immediate family, the estate could go to the state.

In addition, the court has the task of selecting a guardian for your minor children if you fail to name a guardian in a valid will.

Even under the best of circumstances, this process is lengthy. Without estate planning and without a valid will, this situation can be financially and emotionally disastrous for the surviving spouse and children.

PROTECT YOURSELF AND YOUR CHILDREN THROUGH ESTATE PLANNING

Although the word *estate* conjures up the image of wealth, estate planning is for everyone. This process consists of two basic parts:

- Listing one's financial assets and liabilities, determining the likely financial needs of one's heirs, then developing a plan to distribute assets to meet those needs.
- In light of the previously mentioned plan, avoiding expense, delays, and, in some cases, inheritance taxes by transferring property without going through probate court.

How to Transfer Property Without Going Through Probate Court

There are a number of ways to ensure that property can be transferred without going through probate court. Among them are:

1. Joint tenancy or tenancy by entirety. Joint tenancy is a method by which two or more people hold title to property, such as a home, an automobile, or a bank account. All joint tenants own equal interest in the property. In the event one owner dies, the property automatically passes to the other owner or owners without going through probate court. For example, you would have immediate access to money invested in mutual funds or bank certificates of deposit if you and your spouse held them as joint tenants, instead of having the accounts frozen for months, even years, if they are subject to probate proceedings. If there is no will, or the will is declared invalid, you still would possess entire title to the property, instead of to the one-third to one-half share that you would receive under the intestate laws of your state.

Tenancy by entirety, which exists in several states, is a special type of joint tenancy that can exist only between spouses. Unlike joint tenancy, tenancy by entirety cannot be changed by one spouse alone. In other respects, it is identical to joint tenancy.

2. Life insurance. The proceeds of a life insurance policy are paid directly to the beneficiary and are not subject to the jurisdiction of a probate court. Although the owner of a policy can change the beneficiary or even borrow against the policy at any time, payment of the policy cannot be affected by the provisions of the will. If you are the beneficiary of your spouse's insurance policy, you would receive the entire amount even in the absence of a will.

3. Pensions or retirement funds. If your spouse names you as the beneficiary of company pension funds or funds in an IRA or other retirement account, those funds or, in some cases, payouts from funds go to you without going through probate court. If your spouse has not taken the proper steps to legally name you as beneficiary, the funds will be subject to the probate process.

4. Gifts. There is no limit to the property one spouse may give to the other spouse without paying any gift taxes. You also may give up to $10,000 per year to your children or anyone else without paying gift taxes. Some of these gifts may be subject to estate taxes, however, if given within a certain time before the death of the giver.

5. Trusts. A trust is a legal arrangement in which one person holds property for the benefit of another person. For example, money often is placed in trust for children until they reach the age where they can assume control of the money by themselves. Certain kinds of trusts allow a person to enjoy the income from property that will be transferred to the beneficiary without going through probate court.

Obtain Professional Advice Whenever You Make a Major Financial Purchase or Decision

When you purchase a new car, you receive a booklet that provides a detailed service program that every owner should follow. Almost everyone follows the general outline of that program by, for example, routinely changing the oil in their cars to keep them running smoothly and to prevent the destruction of the engines. Generally, everyone understands that spending a reasonable amount of money on oil changes and other kinds of preventative maintenance reduces the risk of very expensive problems occurring in the future.

It is even more essential to protect your financial future and that of your children by consulting a financial planner to develop an estate plan and to ask about the estate implications when making major financial decisions. Among the important reasons are:

- State laws are complicated and vary widely from state to state.
- Every method of transferring property without going through probate court has federal tax consequences.
- Every state has different income, estate, and inheritance tax regulations.
- Estimating the return on investment, the cost of living, and living expenses years in the future is a very complicated task.

You should seek advice when you or your spouse:

- Purchase property to which you take title, including real estate, automobiles, and recreational vehicles.
- Start or purchase a business.
- Register copyrights, trademarks, or patents.
- Open or change retirement accounts.
- Purchase life insurance.
- Receive an inheritance or other financial windfall.
- Have a child.
- Assume financial responsibility for an aging parent or other relative.
- Set money aside to pay for the education of your children.

How to Find a Reputable Financial Planner

A financial planner is an individual who has been trained to design short-term or long-term investment goals for clients, including retirement and estate planning. To date, most good financial planners have been trained as accountants, lawyers, bankers, insurance agents, or stockbrokers. Some colleges now offer formal programs in financial planning.

Although about 250,000 people use the title "financial planner," generally only one in five has sought to validate this professionalism by meeting the requirements for certification by and membership in one or more of five professional registries. These organizations include:

- **Organization:** Institute of Certified Financial Planners
  Designation: C.F.P. (Certified Financial Planner)
  Requirements: Certified Financial Planners must:
  - Complete a two-year, six-part program conducted by the College for Financial Planning. The six parts are:
    - — Introduction to financial planning
    - — Risk management
    - — Investments
    - — Tax planning and management
    - — Retirement planning and employee benefits
    - — Estate planning
  - Pass extensive tests.
  - Meet ethical standards set and enforced by the International Board of Standards and Practices for Certified Financial Planners.
  - Take at least 30 hours of continuing-education instruction each year to keep up to date.

  Publications: *First Steps to Financial Security: A Guide for Selecting a Certified Financial Planner,*
  Financial Planning: Past, Present, and Future, (both free)
  Referral services: Will provide free list of Certified Financial Planners in your area.
  For information: College for Financial Planners
  Institute of Certified Financial Planners
  2 Denver Highlands
  10065 East Harvard Avenue
  Denver, CO 80231
  (800) 282-7526
  (303) 751-7600

- **Organization:** American College
  Designation: Ch.F.C. (Chartered Financial Consultant)
  Requirements: To obtain the designation, individuals must:
  - Have three years' experience as a planner.
  - Pass 10 two-hour examinations.

Referral service: Will provide free list of Chartered Financial Consultants in your area.

For information: American College
270 Bryn Mawr Avenue
Bryn Mawr, PA 19010
(215) 526-1000

▶ **Organization:** International Association for Financial Planning

Designation: R.F.P.P. (Registry of Financial Planning Practitioners)

Requirements: To obtain the designation, individuals must:

- Consider financial planning their major vocation.
- Meet degree requirements related to planning.
- Have at least three years' experience.
- Submit references from five clients.
- Pass a four-hour written examination.
- Participate in continuing-education instruction.

Referral: Publishes a *Directory of Registry Financial Planners* ($2.50). Will provide free referral to practitioners in your area.

For information: International Association for
Financial Planning
2 Concourse Parkway
Atlanta, GA 30328
(404) 395-1605

NOTE: This association has 24,000 members, but only 1,000 have earned the designation R.F.P.P.

▶ **Organization:** International Association of Registered Financial Planners

Designation: R.F.P. (Registered Financial Planner)

Requirements: To earn the designation, individuals must:

- Have a college degree in economics, business, law, or another subject related to financial planning.
- Have passed either a state examination to become an insurance agent or the National Association of Securities Dealers securities examination.

- Have four years' experience.
- Participate in a continuing-education program.

Referral: Will send names of three R.F.P.s in your area on receipt of a self-addressed, stamped envelope.

For information: International Association of Registered Financial Planners
4127 West Cypress Street
Tampa, FL 33607
(813) 875-7352

▶ **Organization:** National Association of Personal Financial Advisors

Designation: None

Requirements: Members must:

- Have education related to financial planning.
- Meet continuing-education requirements.
- Charge clients fees only, not commissions.

Publications: Brochure explaining fee-only planning and a disclosure form to fill out for a prospective planner (free)

Referral: Will provide names, educational backgrounds, and years of experience for members in your area.

For information: National Association of Personal Financial Advisors
1130 Lake Cook Road, Suite 105
Buffalo Grove, IL 60089
(708) 537-7722

In addition to referrals from these organizations, you also should ask for referrals from your lawyer, accountant, credit counselor, or friends with similar financial situations. When you review the backgrounds of all the referrals, you may find that they present one or more of the following additional credentials:

- **C.F.A.** (Chartered Financial Analysts), signifying that the person has passed three very rigorous examinations covering a broad range of investment topics. Successful candidates spend an average of 450 hours studying for the examination, and they must meet rigid ethical standards.

- **C.L.U.** (Chartered Life Underwriter), signifying that the person has completed course work, passed examinations, and acquired the experience necessary to earn this designation as a highly qualified insurance agent. This designation is granted by American College, which also offers the designation Ch.F.C.
- **M.S.F.S.** (Master of Sciences in Financial Services), signifying that the person has completed considerable course work at the American College over and above that necessary to earn the Ch.F.C. designation.
- **J.D.** (Juris Doctor), signifying an attorney
- **C.P.A.** (Certified Public Accountant), signifying a highly trained accountant who has passed very rigorous examinations
- **Registered Investment Adviser.** Any person who provides advice on the purchase of specific securities must register with the Securities and Exchange Commission (SEC). Such registration filters out individuals with criminal records or past violations of securities regulations, but it doesn't indicate that the person possesses any experience or skill.
- **Reg. Rep.** (Registered Representative), signifying that the individual has passed extensive examinations that allow him or her to act as a broker of securities

For more information about selecting a financial planner, write:

▶ **Pamphlet:** *What You Should Know About Financial Planners*
Cost: Free
From: New York State Department of Law
Office of Public Information
120 Broadway
New York, NY 10271

▶ **Booklet:** *How to Talk to and Select: Financial Planners, Lawyers, Tax Preparers, Real Estate Brokers*
Cost: Free
From: AARP
1909 K Street, NW
Washington, DC 20049

PROTECT YOURSELF BY STARTING AND MAINTAINING A VITAL-PAPERS FILE

Every day, well-meaning people create nightmares for their surviving spouses and heirs because they've neglected to leave information as basic as the location of their wills and safe-deposit boxes, the existence of prepaid funeral plans and plots, the existence and policy numbers of insurance policies, and a wealth of other valuable information.

Assembling important information and papers in an estate file is a vital task not only for yourself, but for your parents, in-laws, or other relatives. This estate file should include:

- Names, addresses, and telephone numbers of accountants, tax preparers, lawyers, financial planners, stockbrokers, and other people important to an estate
- A list of all savings and investments, including bank accounts, stocks, bonds, mutual funds, and investment real estate, with account numbers and approximate value
- A list of all debts, with names and addresses of creditors and account numbers
- A list of all important papers, such as income tax returns, birth and marriage certificates, military discharge papers, automobile and home titles, etc., plus the location of the papers
- Complete information about safe-deposit boxes, with inventories of the contents of each box

A valuable workbook that will make this task easier is:

▸ **Workbook:** *Your Vital Papers Logbook*
Cost: $6.95 ($4.95 AARP members) plus $1.75 postage
From: AARP Books/Scott, Foresman and Co.
1865 Miner Street
Des Plaines, IL 60016

PROTECT YOURSELF BY MAKING SURE YOU AND YOUR SPOUSE HAVE WILLS

Wills are vital legal documents for every married couple. By drawing up wills, you and your spouse ensure that both your valuable and sentimental property will be disposed of according to your wishes. Good wills also reduce the time and the costs of the probate process. In their wills, parents also can name the guardian for their children and arrange for the management of their children's finances.

About two-thirds of all adult Americans jeopardize the financial futures of their families by failing to execute legal wills. Yet for the vast majority of couples, drawing up wills is neither a complicated nor an expensive process. Many individual attorneys and legal clinics set the basic price of drawing up a will low as a "loss leader" that attracts new business and encourages clients to appoint the attorney or firm as executors of the estate. Will preparation also is normally included as a membership benefit in the rising number of legal-service plans that offer a variety of services for a low monthly fee. Finally, older Americans can often use free legal services that are available to them.

The cost of having a basic will drawn up by an attorney ranges from $50 to $200. The financial protection and enormous feeling of security derived from having a will makes this a vital step for every couple to take.

How to Purchase Legal Services

Your options include:

1. Joining a legal-service plan. One low-cost, effective option for handling routine legal problems is joining a legal-services plan. In exchange for a membership fee, these plans offer free legal consultation, certain free legal services, and a fixed hourly rate for services not covered by the plan. In addition to will preparation, these plans are valuable in two ways:

- You can ask lawyers for estate-planning advice, to review contracts, to solve consumer problems, and to perform other simple services that you would otherwise not purchase, saving money and preventing problems.
- You save a significant amount of money on the average hourly rate for services purchased, such as incorporating a business.

Many legal-service plans are organized by companies, unions, and other organizations. A number, however, are available to the general public. For a list of these plans and other information, contact:

▶ **Organization:** National Resource Center for Consumers of Legal Services
124-D East Broad Street
Falls Church, VA 22046
(703) 536-8700

---

2. Use a legal clinic. A second option is a legal clinic, a discount law office that advertises heavily on television and in telephone directory listings. These clinics often offer substantial savings and quicker service for routine matters, such as drawing up simple wills and handling real estate closings, uncontested divorces, and simple personal-liability cases, etc. See your telephone directory for listings of legal clinics.

3. Hire a private attorney. A third option is hiring an attorney on your own. Among the sources of referral are:

- Friends and family members
- An attorney-referral service operated by a local bar association or other group (see your telephone directory listing, "Attorney Referral Service")

▶ **Directory:** *Martindale-Hubbell Law Directory*
Contains: A reference book available at most large public libraries that lists the qualifications of attorneys in your community, evaluations of these attorneys by judges and fellow lawyers, and descriptions of their specialties.

For more information on selecting a lawyer:

▶ **Booklet:** *The American Lawyer: How to Choose and Use One*
Cost: $3.00
From: American Bar Association
Information Services
750 North Lake Shore Drive
Chicago, IL 60611
(312) 988-5158

▶ **Publication:** *Money Matters: How to Talk to and Select Lawyers, Financial Planners, Tax Preparers, and Real Estate Brokers*
Cost: Free
From: AARP Fulfillment
1909 K Street, NW
Washington, DC 20049

What About Saving Money by Purchasing Blank Will Forms or Do-It-Yourself Kits?

If your financial affairs are very simple and straightforward, you may be able to prepare a valid will on your own by using forms or other prepackaged materials. But the chances are at least as great that you would create an inadequate or unenforceable document. For your security, you should not give in to the temptation to save money now; instead, have your wills prepared by a competent attorney.

6

Guarding Against Domestic Violence and Your Spouse's Addictions

KEY FACTS

- Domestic violence is one of the most tragic, most common, but least reported of all crimes.
- One out of four American families is affected by drug or alcohol abuse.

Until recent years, the long-established right to marital privacy made even discussions of domestic violence and addictions taboo. And even though the veil that covers these tragedies is slowly being lifted, tens of millions of spouses continue to suffer in silence, often because they have become convinced that they are to blame. The truth is that the spouse who resorts to violence or suffers the addiction is solely responsible. The only moral and legal duty of the other spouse is self-protection.

PROTECT YOURSELF AGAINST DOMESTIC VIOLENCE

Surveys have shown that between 20 and 50 percent of American couples have suffered violence regularly during their marriages. Domestic violence occurs in relationships between people of all ages, including those in the retirement years. Although the vast majority of victims of this violence are women, the percentage of men who are victims increases with age.

The most tragic aspect of domestic violence is that the abused and battered spouse commonly fails to seek help because of feelings of fear, guilt, and shame. These feelings tend to be stronger among Americans who were raised believing in male authority in marriage and that marriages should be held together at all costs. The result is a pattern of violence that can continue for decades.

If your spouse has ever physically abused you or threatened abuse, you must break the pattern by realizing that abuse is a crime. Absolutely no one deserves to be beaten. Every victim is entitled to protection. You are entitled to be protected by:

- **The police.** The majority of American police departments now treat spousal abuse as a serious crime. A growing number of states allow police officers to file criminal charges even if the spouse does not sign a complaint. If you are a victim, you have the right and the duty to call in law-enforcement authorities. Such intervention is necessary, because very few batterers seek help on their own.
- **Battered-women's shelters.** Most larger communities across the United States have shelters where battered women can seek refuge, financial and emotional support, and counseling.
- **The courts.** Battered spouses and ex-spouses have the right to seek a court order of protection that makes it a crime for abusing spouses to enter their homes or workplaces or to approach them in public.

If you are being abused, you should immediately seek help by contacting:

- **Organization:** Local battered-women's shelter
  For information: See your telephone directory listing, "Battered Women"
  or
  call your local Information & Referral Service
  or
  call your local police department.

- **Organization:** National Coalition Against Domestic Violence
  PO Box 15127
  Washington, DC 20036
  (800) 333-7233

  Services: Clearinghouse for information and referral for victims of domestic violence. Can provide information on local services and shelters

- **Organization:** National Women's Abuse Prevention Project
  2000 P Street, NW, Suite 508
  Washington, DC 20036
  (202) 857-0216

  Services: Provides information on preventing domestic abuse

- **Publication:** *Plain Talk About Wife Abuse* (Pub. No. 83-1265)
  Cost: Free
  From: Department of Health and Human Services
  Public Health Service
  Alcohol, Drug Abuse, and Mental Health Administration
  5600 Fishers Lane
  Rockville, MD 20857

If your spouse does indicate a desire to stop committing violence, one support group that can help is:

▶ **Organization:** Batterers Anonymous
1269 North E Street
San Bernardino, CA 92405
(714) 355-1100
Services: Self-help group for men who batter women, modeled on Alcoholics Anonymous

---

PROTECT YOURSELF AGAINST YOUR SPOUSE'S ADDICTIONS

At any given time, one out of every four marriages is being threatened by the alcoholism, drug abuse, or other addiction of one spouse. These addictions take an incredible emotional and financial toll on the other spouse. As with domestic violence (which often goes hand in hand with addiction), the suffering spouse often keeps silent because of guilt, shame, or a feeling of helplessness. Other spouses spend all their time and efforts trying to get their spouses to "change."

If your spouse suffers from an addiction, your first step is to help yourself by getting information and support from one of the following organizations:

▶ **Organization:** Al-Anon Family Groups
Services: Al-Anon is an association of more than 26,000 local self-help groups that offer support and assistance to people whose lives are affected by problem drinkers. Al-Anon publishes many informative books and booklets.

Books:

- *Al-Anon Faces Alcoholism* ($6.00)
- *The Dilemma of the Alcoholic Marriage* ($4.50)
- *One Day at a Time in Al-Anon* (Large Print—$7.50)
- *Al-Anon Family Groups* ($5.00)

Booklets:

- *Al-Anon, You and the Alcoholic* ($ .25)
- *A Guide for the Family of the Alcoholic* ($ .25)
- *Alcoholism: The Family Disease* ($ .50)
- *Alcoholism: A Merry-Go-Round Named Denial* ($ .50)
- *Freedom from Despair* ($ .10)
- *So You Love an Alcoholic* ($ .15)
- *What Do You Do About an Alcoholic's Drinking?* ($ .20)
- *Understanding Ourselves and Alcoholism* ($ .15)
- *Al-Anon Is For Men* ($ .15)
- *"What's Next?" Asks the Husband of an Alcoholic* ($ .30)
- *Does She Drink Too Much?* ($ .40)
- *Al-Anon Is for Adult Children of Alcoholics* ($ .25)

Cost: No postage and handling on prepaid orders
Make checks payable to "AFG, Inc."

For Information: Call your local Al-Anon group (see your telephone directory)

or

Al-Anon Family Group Headquarters
PO Box 862, Midtown Station
New York, NY 10018
(212) 302-7240

▶ **Booklets:**

- *The Alcoholic Spouse* ($ .50)
- *Alcoholics Are Sick People Who Can Be Helped* ($ .25)
- *Dos and Don'ts For Wives of Alcoholics* ($ .50)
- *Intervention* ($1.00)

Cost: Price plus about $1.25 postage and handling

From: National Council on Alcoholism
Publications Manager
12 West 21st Street, Suite 700
New York, NY 10010

▶ **Organization:** Nar-Anon Family Groups
PO Box 2562
Palos Verdes, CA 90274
(213) 547-5800

Services: Support groups for families of drug abusers, modeled on Al-Anon

▶ **Organization:** Gam-Anon
PO Box 157
Whitestone, NY 11357

Services: Support group for families of compulsive gamblers

The emotional support provided by these groups can help you find the strength to take the necessary steps to protect yourself against the financial catastrophes that often are visited on a family by addiction. For example, a spouse who is addicted to drugs or is a compulsive gambler may borrow heavily against marital assets. If your spouse does not seek treatment or admit to having a problem, you should carefully study all the information in this book dealing with financial rights and responsibilities. Then you should consult a lawyer who can help you take legal steps, such as a temporary separation, to protect yourself financially.

7

Protect Your Children's Rights

KEY FACTS

- Marriage does not interfere with a woman's reproductive rights.
- Physical and sexual abuse are increasing threats to America's children.
- Both parents are obligated to support their children. That obligation does not end when parents are divorced or when the parent with custody remarries.
- Illegitimate children now possess almost all the rights that legitimate children do.
- When a child is adopted, he or she receives the same rights as a natural child of the adopting parents or parent.

The decision to have or not have children is a matter of marital privacy and often can cause marital problems. Once a child is born, however, the relationship between parents and child, like the relationship between husband and wife, is accorded a very special legal status in this country. As a parent, you can exercise a great deal of latitude in the way you raise your child, including the freedom to choose the child's religion, standards of behavior, and moral values. You also are responsible for providing that child with food, shelter, clothing, medical care, the opportunity to get an education, and, perhaps most important, love and a sense of security. Your responsibilities last until the child reaches adulthood, and your parent-child relationship lasts for life.

One major legal difference between the husband-wife and the parent-child relationship is that the laws of most states provide for more intervention to protect the child. For example, your state law sets minimum educational standards, prohibits you from leaving the child without responsible supervision, and requires you to provide competent medical care for your child even if that violates your religious beliefs. Courts also take the responsibility for awarding custody in the event of divorce and guardianship in the case of the death of the parents.

Unfortunately, most state agencies and courts are overwhelmed with the number of such cases at a time when the incidence of problems such as domestic violence and child abuse is soaring. While it's impossible to protect children from dangers in society and from the effects of family problems such as divorce, you can make a major difference by acting vigorously to protect your child.

PROTECT YOUR REPRODUCTIVE RIGHTS

Although the courts are extremely reluctant to interfere in the sexual relationship between husband and wife, they have been forced to interpret existing laws when the reproductive rights of the couple come into conflict.

One such conflict involves abortion, perhaps the most incendiary public issue of our times. In the 1973 *Roe v. Wade* decision, the U.S. Supreme Court ruled that every woman had the legal right to an elective abortion during the first trimester of pregnancy. Courts have consistently ruled that a woman's legal right takes precedence over the wishes of the father, whether the couple is married or not. This means that the father cannot legally force a mother to undergo an abortion nor can he legally force her not to undergo an abortion.

Both partners in a marriage also have the right to make their own decisions about contraception. Neither spouse can force the other to undergo surgical sterilization or prevent such a procedure. Although disagreements about whether or not to have children or how many children can be part of "irreconcilable differences" that lead to divorce, such disagreements are not in themselves grounds for divorce.

The only exception is that false claims about having children made before a marriage can be legal grounds for an annulment. For example, a man may promise a woman that they will have children while concealing the fact that he has had a vasectomy. This concealment is grounds for an annulment. Infertility discovered after marriage, however, is not grounds for an annulment.

The best way to protect yourself is to thoroughly discuss with your partner your feelings about having children, about contraception, and about abortion before marriage. Once you are married, you should seek counseling and support should your spouse pressure you about decisions that involve your reproductive rights.

PROTECT YOUR CHILD FROM ABUSE

Physical and sexual abuse are the most terrible of the common forms of violence that can occur within families and other care situations. A survey by the National Institute of Mental Health showed that two million children are the victims of extremely severe violence each year, and 5,000 die as a result. Child abuse is the cause of 10 percent of the hospital emergency-room visits for all children. Studies also show that of all children age 14 and under, one out of every four girls and one out of every six boys have been sexually molested or abused.

The consequences of such abuse can be catastrophic to the

children who are victims. The emotional devastation is compounded by the fact that 30 percent of the abusers are relatives of the victims and an additional 60 percent are babysitters, teachers, neighbors, or other people who the victims know. One of the most important obligations of a parent is to educate yourself about the signs of abuse, teach your children how to protect themselves, and learn what action to take if you suspect abuse has taken place.

The most difficult situation occurs when your spouse or another member of the family is abusing your child. An increasing number of states are emphasizing that the welfare of the child comes first by passing laws requiring criminal prosecution of family members who fail to report such abuse.

Most states and localities have established hot lines that people can call to report suspected cases of child abuse or mistreatment. These hot lines guarantee anonymity to the callers. To obtain the number for your area, check your telephone directory, call your local police department, or call one of these national hot lines:

- **Hot line:** Child Abuse Hot Line: (800) 792-8610
  Services: Provides information and referral 24 hours a day

- **Hot line:** Child Help National Child Abuse Hot Line: (800) 422-4453
  Services: Provides information and referral, including a free publication, "Child Abuse and You"

For information about child abuse, contact:

- **Organization:** Clearinghouse on Child Abuse and Neglect: (301) 251-5157

Services: This office of the federal Department of Health and Human Services provides information, statistics, and referrals to local agencies.

▶ **Organization:** National Committee for the Prevention of Child Abuse
332 South Michigan Avenue, Suite 950
Chicago, IL 60604
(312) 663-3520

Services: National clearinghouse for information and services to abused children and abusing parents. Publishes dozens of valuable booklets and books and provides a free catalog of these publications.

▶ **Booklet:** *Take Time Out to Be a Better Parent and Prevent Child Abuse*
Cost: Free
From: The National Exchange Club Foundation for the Prevention of Child Abuse
3050 Central Avenue
Toledo, OH 43606

Because of the enormous stresses involved with parenting today, it is not uncommon that parents may fear that they, themselves, could abuse their own children. If you have ever experienced such fears, or if you suspect that you may have gone too far in disciplining your children, you should immediately obtain the professional help and support available from:

▶ **Organization:** Parents Anonymous
6733 South Sepulveda Boulevard
Los Angeles, CA 90045
(800) 421-0353 (except in California)
(213) 410-9732

PROTECT YOUR CHILDREN'S BIRTHRIGHTS

Every child born today has legal rights, including:

- The right to be provided with the necessities of life by both parents
- The right to inherit property from both parents
- The right to sue for damages for wrongful death in the event of the death of a parent

In our more enlightened society, the centuries-old legal distinction between "legitimate" and "illegitimate" children has been generally eliminated. Legal action to establish paternity has been made much easier by the development of sophisticated blood tests. At the same time, other new medical procedures such as artificial insemination have somewhat clouded many people's concepts of what a father is. This is why it is more important than ever to protect children by legally establishing who their parents are.

Who Is the Father?

Although state laws can vary, the legal father of a child is generally considered to be a man who meets one of the following criteria:

- Was married to the mother at the time of birth or within 300 days of the time of birth. In some states, the husband is the legal father even if blood tests and other evidence make a strong case that another man is the biological father.
- Was married to the mother of a child conceived through artificial insemination, even if he is not the donor of the sperm
- Acknowledged paternity in writing
- Consented to have his name appear on and has his name appear on the child's birth certificate
- Took the child into his home and refers to the child as his
- Adopted the child in a legal proceeding

- Was declared the child's father as the result of a paternity action

If a man does not acknowledge that he is the father, the mother or, in some cases, state welfare officials, can file a paternity action in a court of law. In such actions, courts have increasingly relied on a blood test known as the Human Leukocyte Antigen (HLA) test. The results of this test can completely eliminate a man as the possible biological father and can establish with a more than 98 percent degree of certainty that a man is the father. In the absence of other incontrovertible evidence (such as proof that the father was stationed overseas in the military or was in prison at the time of conception), the courts usually rely on the test results.

Who Is the Mother?

The legal mother of a child is either the woman who gave birth to the child or the woman who adopted the child in a legal proceeding. Only in a relative handful of cases involving surrogate motherhood have disputes over who is the legal mother reached the courts.

How Long Do Parental Responsibilities Last?

The responsibility of parents to provide the necessities of life for their children can terminate in only one of three ways:

- When the child reaches adulthood (either age 18 or 21, depending on the state). Many state laws, however, make parents responsible for supporting certain mentally or physically handicapped children for life.
- When the child is "emancipated" or freed from parental control. Entering military service automatically emancipates a child, as does marriage in most states. A minor who moves out of the home must be declared emancipated by a

court. Neither a child nor parents can arbitrarily end the parent-child relationship.
- When parental rights are terminated by the court because of adoption. In cases of child neglect, the court may temporarily suspend parental rights and place the child in foster care. Eventually, parental rights are either restored or permanently ended when the child is placed for adoption.

Parental responsibilities exist independent of marital status. An unwed father and a divorced father both have the legal obligation to support a child.

What Are the Responsibilities of a Stepparent?

In recent years, many states have passed laws that make a stepparent responsible for providing necessities to a spouse's children from a previous marriage who live in his or her home. The purpose of these laws was to protect children who were not receiving child support from the noncustodial parent. As discussed in Chapter 1, providing financially for children from a previous marriage is one important purpose of a prenuptial agreement. The obligation of a stepparent to provide support for these children normally ends if there is a separation, divorce, or a change in the custodial status of the children. Stepchildren possess no right of inheritance.

Can a Stepparent Adopt a Spouse's Child?

Such adoptions are routine if the noncustodial parent is dead or, in the case of an unwed mother, no determination of paternity was ever made. Normally, the courts are cautious about terminating the parental rights of a living noncustodial parent. A hearing will be held at which that parent can present arguments against such an adoption. The court generally will grant an adoption under two circumstances:

- The noncustodial parent agrees to the adoption.

- The noncustodial parent can't be located or doesn't respond to the notice of the hearing and has had no contact with the child for a significant period of time, such as five years.

When such an adoption takes place, the parents can petition the court to change the child's last name to the stepparent's name. The parents will be required to prove that the name change will be beneficial to the child, rather than just being a matter of convenience.

What Are the Rights of an Adopted Child?

A child that has been legally adopted possesses all the rights of a natural child, including the right to support and the right to inherit. The only way these rights can be terminated is if the court cancels the adoption during the six- to eighteen-month trial period after the adoption takes place.

A child who is adopted normally has no claim for support or inheritance from the biological parents.

PROTECT YOUR CHILDREN FINANCIALLY DURING MARRIAGE

Protecting your children financially during marriage consists of two basic steps:

1. Providing for their support in the event of your death and/or the death of your spouse.
2. Safeguarding their financial assets.

Providing for Your Children After the Death of One or Both Parents

The most important step you can take to protect your children is for you and your spouse to draw up valid wills. In your will, you can name a guardian for your children and list the property that you want your children to inherit. If your children are minors, you can appoint a trustee to manage their money and property until they reach a certain age.

In addition, both you and your spouse may well need to take out life insurance policies if the income from your estate will not support your children. For example, the conservatively invested proceeds of a $100,000 life insurance policy would provide an income of $500 to $600 per month for a child. The principal also could be used for college expenses.

When planning for the support of your children, you may need to obtain the advice of a financial professional (see Chapter 4).

Managing Your Child's Money

Generally, you are responsible for the financial affairs of your minor children. Your children cannot enter into a valid contract without your signature, nor can they make out wills. Because you are responsible for providing a child's support, you are entitled to any wages the child earns from employment. Although most parents allow their children to spend their own earnings, you are legally entitled to spend that money any way that you see fit.

However, parents are not entitled to spend an inheritance, a gift of money, money awarded by a legal judgment, or any other financial windfall that their children receive. Instead, parents are expected to manage such money prudently in trust for the child. Because supporting the child is the parents' responsibility, income from investments cannot be used to pay for the necessities of life. A court may approve using the income from the investments for special needs, such as unusual educational or medical expenses, but very rarely will the court grant permission to use the principal.

One of the rude shocks that can occur during a divorce is discovering that a spouse spent or imprudently invested a child's money. To protect your children, you should ensure that their money is invested safely and you should regularly check statements to ensure that the money hasn't been touched. If misappropriation has occurred, your child can file suit to recover the funds.

PROTECT YOUR CHILD DURING SEPARATION AND DIVORCE

Children often suffer the most when a marriage is crumbling or when it ends. The welfare of children is such a social priority that state law gives the courts the final responsibility to award custody and mandate child-support payments. The courts, however, cannot watch over a child on a day-to-day basis. As a parent, you can do a great deal to protect your children emotionally, financially, and physically during separation and divorce. Because protecting your children is intertwined with protecting yourself, this subject will be discussed in detail in the next chapter.

8

What You Need to Know About Annulment, Separation, and Divorce

KEY FACTS

- More than one out of every two marriages will end in annulment or divorce, and half of these will end within seven years of the wedding day.
- An annulment is a judgment by the court that the marriage never existed. Most annulments are granted when one spouse lies or misleads the other about an important factor to the marriage.
- Couples who wish to live apart can obtain a judicial separation, an official court decree, or can separate by agreement between themselves. In either case, separation is a legal status in which many marital rights and responsibilities are changed.
- All 50 states have "no-fault" divorce laws. Proof of fault is required in many states when a divorce is contested, and this proof may affect such elements of the divorce settlement as property division, child custody, child support, and alimony.

The U.S. Census Bureau has estimated that as many as half of all current marriages will lead to annulment or divorce. These marriages will, in fact, have two ends—one emotional, the other legal and financial. The end of the romantic union between husband and wife almost always produces emotions ranging from depression to rage. These emotions further complicate the already complex process of ending the marriage legally and financially.

Ending your marriage inevitably will take a toll on you and your children. You cannot expect to be always calm, always rational, always reasonable during the process. By taking certain important precautions, however, you can expect to significantly reduce the impact on yourself and on your children.

PROTECT YOURSELF BY SEEKING AN ANNULMENT

An annulment is a declaration by the court that a marriage never existed. Before the enactment of "no-fault" laws that made divorces much easier to obtain, annulments were much more common. Today, between 1 and 2 percent of marriages are annulled.

What Are the Grounds for an Annulment?

To obtain an annulment, a spouse must prove that one of the following conditions existed at the time of the wedding:

1. Fraud. Among the common types of deception accepted as grounds for annulment are:

- Concealing an existing marriage
- Concealing a previous divorce or children
- Concealing homosexuality
- Concealing impotence
- Concealing a serious health problem or addiction

- Concealing pregnancy by another man
- False claims of pregnancy
- False claims of wanting to have children

2. Duress. An annulment can be granted if one spouse was forced into marriage by threats of violence or blackmail.

3. Mental incapacity. An annulment can be granted if one spouse was not mentally capable of understanding the full implications of marriage. This incapacity can result from mental retardation, senility, serious illness, or intoxication from alcohol or drugs.

4. Under age. A person who was under the required legal age at the time of marriage cannot be held to have consented to the marriage.

5. Inability to consummate the marriage. An annulment can be granted on these grounds even if fraud did not occur.

What Are the Advantages of an Annulment?

An annulment erases the existence of a marriage. In some cases, annulment restores a person's right to receive alimony from an ex-spouse or to become eligible for Social Security benefits based on the earnings record of an ex-spouse. After an annulment, both spouses are immediately free to marry.

Although an annulment voids a marriage, any children from that marriage still are considered legitimate. Annulment decrees, like divorce decrees discussed later in this chapter, can include provisions for property division, child custody, child support, and alimony.

What Is the Procedure for Seeking an Annulment?

In addition to proving you have grounds for an annulment,

you also must meet three basic requirements. You can begin the annulment process only when you discover that you have legal grounds. For example, you can file for an annulment if you discover that your spouse is a homosexual. You will not be granted an annulment, however, if you knew of the homosexuality at the time of the marriage.

Second, your petition for an annulment in certain states must be filed within a certain time period after the marriage. For example, a state may require that you seek an annulment within one year if you are using failure to consummate the marriage as grounds. If you fail to file during the statutory period, you must seek a divorce instead.

Third, you must seek an annulment promptly after learning that fraud took place. If you wait two years to seek an annulment after learning that your spouse is an alcoholic, for instance, the court may decline to grant your request because you have accepted the fraud.

If you meet all these requirements, you should retain the services of a competent attorney. Although the legal process of seeking an annulment differs somewhat from the processes of legal separation and divorce, you will need the same assistance to protect yourself and your children when negotiating the terms of the end of the marriage.

Does a Legal Annulment Allow a Catholic to Remarry?

No. Catholics or members of other religions that prohibit remarriage after divorce must seek a religious annulment before remarrying in their religion.

PROTECT YOURSELF DURING SEPARATION

Becoming separated means that a couple has decided not to live together, either temporarily or permanently. You must understand that separation is a legal status that must be accomplished in accordance with the laws of your state. Although the term often conjures up the image of one spouse storming out of the house or throwing the other spouse out, both of these acts can be considered abandonment, legal grounds for divorce that could adversely affect the court's decisions about child custody and the division of marital property. This is one reason why the decision to separate should not be made in anger.

Legally, two types of marital separation exist: judicial separation and separation by agreement.

What Is Judicial Separation?

Judicial separation is the result of a judicial decree issued after a process that is virtually identical to the process of obtaining a legal divorce. To obtain a judicial separation, one spouse petitions the court, stating legal grounds that are valid grounds for divorce in that state. The court holds hearings on the petition and issues a decree that awards custody of the children, divides marital property, and establishes any child-support or alimony payments. The major difference between judicial separation and divorce is that the marriage is not ended and the husband and wife are not free to remarry.

People normally seek judicial separation for one of three reasons:

1. One spouse refuses to agree to a separation.
2. The couple will not consider obtaining a divorce for religious, moral, or other reasons.
3. The couple has not resided in a state long enough to meet residency requirements for filing for divorce.

What Is Separation by Agreement?

Because the process of obtaining a judicial separation virtually duplicates the divorce process, most couples legally separate by negotiating an agreement that covers the terms of the separation. Legal separation primarily changes a couple's financial relationship. Each spouse's income normally is considered separate rather than marital property, and all debts incurred are normally separate debts. The only exceptions are debts incurred for the necessities of life, such as food, housing, clothing, and medical care.

Many states require that the agreement be in writing before the separation is legal. Even in states without such a law, written agreements are vital because oral agreements are difficult, if not impossible, to enforce.

One major advantage of separating by agreement is that the process is less time-consuming, less complicated, and less expensive than judicial separation. Separation agreements are legally enforceable contracts. Although holding a spouse to the terms of a separation agreement is more complicated than enforcing a court decree, judges often mandate stiffer terms in final divorce settlements to spouses who violate separation agreements.

How to Protect Yourself While Separating from Your Spouse

The decision to separate often is more emotional than the decision to go ahead with the divorce. You and your children are most vulnerable at this time, so you must take the following steps to protect yourself:

1. Retain the services of a professional, whether you are seeking a judicial separation or a separation by agreement, for the following reasons:

- State laws concerning separation can be very technical. Without the advice of a professional attorney, you may unwittingly give up important rights.
- Communication between husband and wife tends to be at its absolute worst just prior to separation, which makes it even more difficult to negotiate an equitable agreement.

If you are seeking a judicial separation or if your relationship with your spouse is adversarial or hostile, you should retain the services of an attorney. If you are worried about paying legal fees, you should discuss the subject during your initial consultation with an attorney. In many cases, you can ask the court to order your spouse to pay your legal fees as a part of the settlement. If you and your spouse have modest means, you can contact your local Legal Aid Society to see if you are eligible for free legal assistance. Even if you are not eligible, the society usually can direct you to attorneys who charge reasonable fees.

An increasing number of couples who want to conclude the separation proceedings without acrimony are saving considerable money by using the services of an impartial mediator to reach a settlement. For information about mediation contact:

▸ **Organization:** The Academy of Family Mediators
PO Box 10501
Eugene, OR 97440
(503) 345-1205

Services: Provides referrals to mediators who meet its strict standards

▸ **Organization:** American Arbitration Association
140 West 51st Street
New York, NY 10020

Services: Provides services described in a free brochure, "Family Mediation Rules"

---

2. Provide your attorney or the mediator with complete information. During your first consultation, you should provide the following:

- A copy of your marriage license
- The names and the dates of the births of your children and

any other dependents, such as an elderly parent

- A copy of any prenuptial or marital agreements
- A listing of your marital property, including real estate, automobiles, furniture, appliances, artwork, collections, electronic equipment
- A complete list, with account numbers, of joint bank accounts, certificates of deposit, stocks and bonds, retirement accounts, money-market funds, etc.
- A listing of your separate property, including jewelry, bank accounts, investments, real estate, etc.
- As complete a listing as possible of your spouse's separate property
- A list of all joint and separate debts, including mortgages, credit-card balances, car loans, etc.
- Copies of your joint tax returns for the past two or three years
- Copies of tax returns for your business or the business operated with your spouse
- A list of health, life, disability, homeowners, automobile, and other insurance policies

The more complete information your attorney or mediator has, the better qualified he or she will be to negotiate a separation agreement that covers:

- Who will pay financial support and how much will be paid
- Who will live in the family home and other residences
- A detailed monthly budget of all expenses, from mortgage or rent payments to child care and school lunches
- Who will have use of other property, such as furniture, automobiles, appliances, electronic equipment, etc.
- Custody and support of the children, as well as visitation rights for the noncustodial spouse
- Who will pay insurance premiums and exactly what coverage will be retained
- Who will pay every joint or separate debt
- Who is responsible for filing income tax returns and how refunds will be dispersed
- What rights each of you have to inherit from the other, should a death occur before a divorce

3. Secure your joint assets, especially bank accounts, money-market funds, stocks and bonds, the contents of safe-deposit boxes, and any other property readily convertible to cash. It is not unusual for a spouse to attempt to empty such accounts before a separation agreement can be negotiated. As soon as it becomes apparent that a separation is going to take place, you should consult your attorney on what immediate action you can take to secure access to these funds.

4. Limit your liability for any debt incurred by your spouse. In most cases, this means canceling all joint credit cards, charge accounts, and personal credit lines. This may cause some hardship if you don't have sufficient credit in your own name or have never established credit in your own name. If you need access to certain joint credit cards or accounts, you should have your attorney or the mediator include a provision in the separation agreement.

5. Avoid confrontations with your spouse. The worst thing you can do is to get involved in violent arguments or even retaliatory actions should your spouse violate your separation agreement. You never know when your response could be used against you in the divorce proceedings. Instead of being provoked when your spouse is late with a support payment, you should positively channel your feelings by keeping careful records of any such violations of the separation agreement.

6. Live up to the terms and the spirit of your separation agreement. The process of ending a marriage is always adversarial. You are more likely to keep bad feelings from escalating, however, if you adhere to the terms of your separation agreement and attempt to be fair when, inevitably, situations arise that are not covered by the separation agreement.

7. Be prudent about relationships with the opposite sex. During the separation process you still are legally married. You can date, but you should avoid serious or long-term relationships that could be used as grounds for divorce or used against you in awarding custody of your children.

8. Avoid extravagant spending. Although the desire to treat yourself to luxuries during this emotionally trying time may be strong, you can benefit only from acting responsibly before the separation or divorce proceedings.

9. Get counseling for yourself and your children. Some states require that couples undergo marital counseling before a separation or divorce will be granted. If your state doesn't require counseling, you should take the initiative and arrange counseling for yourself, even if you're convinced you are handling the situation well.

Arranging counseling for your children is even more important. Children whose parents are separating or divorcing can react in many different ways, ranging from serious depression to rebellion at school. You and your spouse should participate in this counseling as much as possible, and share the expense as well.

One way to locate qualified counselors in your area is to contact:

▸ **Organization:** American Association for Marriage and Family Therapy
1717 K Street, NW, Suite 407
Washington, DC 20006

Services: Will provide referrals to member therapists who specialize in the problems connected with separation or divorce (send self-addressed, stamped envelope)

If you are worried about the cost of counseling, you can obtain information about free or low-cost services that are available by contacting your community mental-health center (see your telephone directory listing, "Mental Health") or consult your state government listings for the number of your state Department of Mental Health.

PROTECT YOURSELF DURING DIVORCE

A divorce is the legal ending of a marriage, as well as the termination of all marital rights and responsibilities for the husband and wife. The financial and emotional effects of divorce, however, can last much, much longer. If the couple had children, their relationship as parents continues for life.

Because divorce has such complex ramifications, you owe it to yourself and to your children to understand the process completely and to continue to act in your best interest during and after the divorce proceedings.

What Is the Procedure for Filing for Divorce?

Either spouse can file for divorce, providing that the filing spouse meets the residency requirements of the state in which one of the spouses lives. If the custody of the children will be involved in the divorce, the proceedings normally take place in the state in which the children live. Alaska, South Dakota, and Washington have no residency requirement. The requirement in other states ranges from six weeks to one year, with the average being six months. There are no residency requirements for a legal separation.

The days when one spouse could dash off to a foreign country and return with a surprise divorce are over. Today, foreign divorces generally are not recognized as legal unless the spouse filing for divorce has met the residency requirements of the foreign country, and both partners consent to the divorce.

Once residency requirements have been met, divorce proceedings may be initiated by filing the appropriate documents (usually called a "Petition for Divorce" or "Divorce Complaint") with the appropriate court. On the petition, you will be asked to provide basic information about the marriage, such as the names and birth dates of you and your spouse, the date of your marriage, the names and ages of any children, and the grounds on which you are basing the petition.

If you and your spouse have not agreed on a working separation agreement, you also may file papers asking the court to issue temporary orders granting you financial support, possession of your home, custody and support of your children, or protection from your spouse. Your requests will be acted on at a preliminary hearing.

Finally, you will fill out a notice that will be served on your spouse by a marshal or process server. This notice will give your spouse a certain time period, normally 30 days, to respond to your petition. If you do not know where your spouse is, you must make reasonable efforts to inform him or her. These efforts could include placing a notice in the local newspaper, contacting relatives, or calling an employer.

If your spouse files a response, the court normally provides a period of time for both parties to negotiate a divorce settlement. If either party is dissatisfied with the other's openness about financial assets and liabilities, the court will order "discovery," a process in which both parties must produce documents and records requested by the other and submit to questioning officially transcribed by a court reporter. In approximately nine out of ten divorces, a negotiated settlement is reached and a final hearing date is set by the court. In the remaining cases, the settlement will be decided by a judge or a jury after a trial is held.

If your spouse fails to respond, you can ask the court to make an official entry of default. If the default is granted, your divorce will proceed uncontested, and such issues as division of property and child custody will be decided on the basis of the laws of your state and the discretion of the judge.

In some states, the judge will issue a final order of divorce at the conclusion of the final hearing or trial. In other states, the divorce takes place in two stages. The first, called the interlocutory stage, involves an order that settles all the issues in the divorce, such as division of property, child custody and support, alimony, and other issues. Then there is a waiting period, which ranges from two to six months and is designed to give couples another chance to reconcile. At the conclusion of this waiting period, the final divorce decree that ends the marriage will be issued.

What Are the Legal Grounds for Divorce?

Until 1970, the spouse seeking a divorce was forced to prove that the other spouse was guilty of serious marital misconduct, such as adultery, abandonment, or physical or mental cruelty, before a divorce could be granted. This requirement resulted in widespread perjury as couples who wanted to divorce concocted "evidence" of misconduct. Over the past two decades, all 50 states have recognized that couples should be allowed to decide if their marriage is over by enacting no-fault divorce laws.

These no-fault laws allow a divorce to be granted on one or both of the following grounds:

- "Irreconcilable differences," "irretrievable breakdown," or similar terms that indicate the couple can no longer continue the marriage
- A legal separation for a period of time ranging from six months to five years

The vast majority of divorces today are issued on the basis of these no-fault grounds.

Thirty-four states, however, still allow divorces to be filed on one or more grounds of serious marital misconduct. These grounds include:

- Adultery
- Physical cruelty
- Mental cruelty
- Abandonment or desertion for a certain length of time
- Bigamy
- Insanity, normally proved by confinement to a mental institution
- Imprisonment for at least a year
- Alcoholism or drug abuse

Before you file for divorce, you should thoroughly discuss the grounds with your attorney. In some states, courts can issue no-fault divorces even if the other spouse contests the action. In other states, grounds must be changed from "no fault" to "fault" if the action is contested. Finally, in some states, proving certain types of marital misconduct can affect the way in which judges make financial and child-custody decisions.

What Is the Procedure if You Have Previously Obtained a Judicial Separation?

If you have been granted a judicial separation, you and your spouse can save time and expense by having that separation "converted" into a divorce. If the petition is not contested, the granting of a converted divorce is normally routine.

How Will Your Property Be Divided?

Some of the important steps you can take to achieve a fair property settlement must take place long before your divorce. These steps include negotiating a fair and valid prenuptial agreement, safeguarding your separate property, prudently managing your marital finances, consulting a professional about the estate implications of major financial decisions, and protecting your children's finances. In addition, a fair and detailed written separation agreement is an excellent basis for a divorce settlement.

If you and your spouse present an agreement on the division of your marital property and debts to the court, the judge normally will review the settlement to ensure that it:

- Conforms to state laws about the division of property
- Conforms to any legally enforceable provisions of a prenuptial agreement
- Has been arrived at fairly and without coercion or deception

If you and your spouse have not reached an agreement, the judge will divide the property in accordance with state law and at the judge's own discretion.

As discussed in Chapter 2, state laws treat the division of marital property in one of two ways:

- In the community-property states (see page 19), each spouse is entitled to one-half of all marital property. In some of these states, the judge may modify this requirement when one partner is found at fault or is guilty of economic misconduct.
- In all other states (except Mississippi), the judge is allowed to make an "equitable distribution" of the marital property. In making such a distribution, the judge considers such factors as:
    - The length of the marriage
    - The spouses' occupations and abilities to find jobs
    - The spouses' incomes from employment and other sources
    - The standard of living and need of each spouse
    - The amount each spouse contributed to the purchase and maintenance of marital property
    - The nonmonetary contributions of each spouse, such as homemaking and child care
    - The expenses for the spouse with custody of the children
    - The loss of potential pension and other retirement income
- In Mississippi, property goes to the spouse whose name is on the title. Property held jointly is divided equally.

Debts also are divided in line with the property settlement and the means of each spouse to repay the debt. This division, however, does not end your liability for joint debts. A creditor legally can seek payment from you in the event that your ex-spouse defaults on a joint debt that he or she was ordered to pay as part of the divorce settlement. Your only recourse would be to take legal action against your ex-spouse to recover the money. The creditor also may seek payment from you after the death of your ex-spouse. To protect yourself, try to include in the settlement a provision that such debts would be paid by your ex-spouse's estate or a provision that your ex-spouse must make you the beneficiary of life insurance in an amount sufficient to pay off such debts.

If you and your spouse have any significant assets, you must use the services of a competent attorney or mediator to negotiate a fair settlement. State laws can be very technical, and you may find yourself negotiating away rights and assets that the court would otherwise grant you. You also would find it difficult to calculate the present and future tax obligations that result from the property settlement.

How Is Alimony Determined?

In the past, the courts routinely ordered the ex-husband to make alimony payments to his ex-wife for life, especially if he were at fault in the divorce. Today, when two-income couples are the rule, not the exception, the awarding of alimony is less common. When a court orders such payments, which now are often called "spousal support" or "spousal maintenance," these payments frequently last only for a specific period of time instead of for life.

The most common form of spousal support today is called "rehabilitative support." The purpose of these payments is to allow the spouse who was economically disadvantaged by the marriage to learn or regain job skills and find suitable employment. This support normally lasts for a short period of time, such as three years. In some states, the period can be extended if the spouse receiving support has trouble finding a job. In almost all cases, this support immediately ends when the recipient remarries.

"Permanent support" normally is ordered when the court finds that it is unlikely that the recipient could ever find employment that would allow the recipient to maintain a reasonable standard of living. Some states consider fault in the decision either to award alimony or deny alimony. In almost every case, alimony ends with the remarriage of the recipient.

You should understand two important facts about alimony. The first is that alimony payments are tax deductible to the payer and taxable to the recipient. For this reason, many spouses prefer to forgo alimony in favor of a larger property settlement, because property transfers between husband and wife are not taxable. Others prefer larger child-support payments, which are not taxable to the recipient.

The second important fact is that alimony payments normally cease with the death of the payer, and the recipient has no claim against the ex-spouse's estate. For this reason, most settlements that include alimony payments also require the payer to make the recipient the beneficiary of a life insurance policy large enough to protect against that eventuality.

How Does the Court Award Child Custody?

Custody includes both physical control over a child and the legal authority to make medical, educational, spiritual, and other decisions affecting the welfare of the child. In the past, the custody of children was routinely awarded to the mother, and visitation rights were given to the father. Today, courts are more willing to consider other custodial options, including joint custody.

An increasing number of states are authorizing or encouraging joint custody, which can consist of one or two options:

- Joint legal custody, in which both parents share the legal authority to make decisions even though one parent has physical custody of the child
- Joint physical custody, in which parents share both legal and physical custody. In this situation, the child may spend half the week at one parent's home and half at the other's, alternate months between parents' homes, or another similar arrangement.

Courts will not allow a couple to include provisions about child custody in prenuptial agreements, and they closely examine any custodial agreement made between a divorcing couple. The best interests of each child is the overriding consideration in awarding custody. A major concern is providing stability in a child's life by keeping him or her in the same home, school, and community. The judge considers past parental involvement in child rearing as well as which parent is better able and more willing to meet the child's physical and emotional needs. Each parent's mental and physical health are factors. Finally, the judge considers the preferences of older children.

The increase in two-career households has complicated the decision to award custody. In a still small but increasing number of divorces, custody is awarded to the father because the mother travels a great deal on business or continually places a higher priority on her career rather than on family responsibilities. Custody decisions also are strongly affected by parental behavior, such as alcoholism, drug abuse, instability in relationships, and other actions that could adversely affect a child.

To protect your rights to the custody of your children, you should:

- Make the stability of your children's lives a priority. You may want to move out of your home or even move to another city to make a new start. The court, however, may prefer that you make decisions based on what's best for your children.
- Act vigorously to protect your children. The effects of divorce may show up first outside of the home. You should be able to show the court that you have been in frequent contact with teachers, coaches, day-care directors, parents of your children's friends, and others who may be able to alert you to problems.
- Act responsibly in both your financial and personal lives.
- Don't use visitation rights as a weapon against your spouse, even if you feel you have been provoked. Courts in every state place a high priority on maintaining children's relationships with both parents.

How Do Courts Award Child Support?

Even after a divorce, both parents continue to share the responsibility to support their children, no matter which parent has custody. Custody does, however, make a difference in how that responsibility is carried out. In most cases, the noncustodial parent is ordered by the court to pay monthly child support to the custodial parent until the child has become an adult or has been emancipated. Among the factors involved in setting the amount of these payments are:

- The assets, income, and needs of both parents
- The ages and needs of the children
- Any special educational, emotional, or medical needs of the children
- The standard of living the children would have attained had the marriage not ended

In addition, the noncustodial parent may be required to pay for some or all of the other important expenses, such as college or private-school tuition, bills for tutoring or other special instruction, or major medical or dental expenses.

The responsibility of the parent who has custody is to use the child-support payments solely for the benefit of the children. Judges tend to deal harshly with parents who misuse child-support money.

You can take two important steps while negotiating your divorce settlement to protect your children's child-support payments. First, you should insist that your ex-spouse maintain sufficient life insurance to compensate for the loss of child-support payments. As with alimony, child support normally terminates with the death of your ex-spouse.

Second, you should insist that your ex-spouse's child-support payments be made to the court, which will, in turn, pass on the money to you. Court records are the best proof should you have to take action against your ex-spouse for nonpayment of child support.

Can Alimony, Child-Custody, and Child-Support Stipulations Be Changed in Future Years?

A divorce settlement is never final. Both you and your ex-spouse have the right to go back to the court to petition for a change in or elimination of alimony and child-support payments, as well as a change in child custody.

In most cases, the court must be convinced that there is a compelling reason to modify alimony and child-support payments. Normally, these requests are not granted without presenting convincing evidence of financial hardship. For example, you may ask for an increase in child-support payments after learning that your ex-spouse took a new job at a much higher salary or received some other type of financial windfall. This request probably would not be granted unless you could convince the judge that the present level of payments was causing financial hardship. Similarly, your ex-spouse would not be allowed to reduce child-support payments when your income increased without proving that the present level of payments was causing your ex-spouse severe financial hardship.

Even more compelling proof normally is needed to reverse child-custody decisions. Such proof would include evidence of child abuse, child neglect, or serious misconduct such as alcohol or drug abuse on the part of the custodial parent. For example, it is unlikely that your ex-spouse could obtain custody simply because he or she remarried, or because he or she experienced a dramatic increase in income.

However, you should protect yourself and your children by immediately retaining a competent attorney if your ex-spouse seeks a change in the divorce settlement, no matter how frivolous that request seems. You also should not hesitate to retain an attorney to seek a change in the divorce settlement if the present levels of support are resulting in provable financial hardship.

How Can You Obtain Help in Coping with Divorce and Getting on with Your Life?

As discussed previously, professional counseling can play a crucial role in helping you and your children cope with the ending of a marriage. A number of support groups also can provide vital information as well as a shoulder to lean on when you need it. These groups include:

▶ **Organization:** Displaced Homemakers Network
1010 Vermont Avenue, NW
Washington, DC 20005
(202) 628-6767

Services: A coalition of local groups that provides a wide range of information and services for women who are on their own

▶ **Organization:** Older Women's League
1325 G Street, NW
Washington, DC 20005

Services: Through local chapters, an organization that provides information, support groups, and services

▶ **Organization:** Women's Legal Defense Fund
2000 P Street, NW, Suite 400
Washington, DC 20036
(202) 887-0364

Services: An organization that provides information and publications on women's legal problems, including those associated with divorce

▶ **Organization:** Parents Without Partners
460 Park Avenue South
New York, NY 10016

Services: A self-help group for single parents of both sexes

▶ **Organization:** North American Conference of Separated and Divorced Catholics
1100 South Goodman Street
Rochester, NY 14620
(716) 271-1320

Services: A self-help group, open to people of all religions, that has more than 3,000 local groups

9

Enforcing Court Orders After a Divorce

KEY FACTS

- Divorce does not always end domestic violence.
- New federal laws provide more protection for the custodial spouse.
- Because only half of all court-ordered child-support payments are made in full and on time, new federal laws will require such payments to be automatically deducted from the wages of the noncustodial spouse.
- Courts can take a wide variety of actions, including contempt citations, when court-ordered alimony is not paid.

Divorce often does not end the relationship between ex-spouses. Violence against ex-spouses, custody battles, and failure to pay court-ordered child support and alimony have become so common that these acts have been called a national scandal. Fortunately, new federal and state laws have been enacted that offer you and your children significant new protections if you are divorced.

PROTECT YOURSELF PHYSICALLY FROM YOUR EX-SPOUSE

Divorce frequently fails to end domestic violence. If you or your children were physically or emotionally abused by your ex-spouse during your marriage, you should obtain a court order of protection along with your divorce decree. This decree makes it a crime for your ex-spouse to even approach your home. You should carry a copy of this order at all times and call the local police should it be violated.

Violations of an order of protection and verbal threats are grounds for limiting or eliminating an ex-spouse's visitation rights. You should not hesitate to bring these situations to the attention of the court immediately after they occur.

Divorce also ends your ex-spouse's conjugal rights. Any attempt to force sexual activity is legally considered rape. You owe it to yourself to report any rape attempts or violence to the police.

Finally, you should take action if your ex-spouse gives any indication of not honoring a court order of protection. The best course of behavior is to immediately contact your local battered-women's shelter (see Chapter 6) so that you and your children can be fully protected.

PROTECT YOUR RIGHTS TO CUSTODY OF YOUR CHILDREN

In a small but troubling number of divorces, the dispute over custody of the children does not end with the court decree. In the past, the bitter noncustodial spouse would take the child or children involved after obtaining a different custodial decision in another state. With state courts in conflict, the original custodial spouse faced an expensive, difficult process to regain custody, partially because legal jurisdiction was so clouded.

Fortunately, these legal problems ended when all 50 states and the District of Columbia enacted the Uniform Child Custody Jurisdiction Act. Essentially, this act mandated that the original child-custody decision cannot be modified or contradicted by the courts in any other state. It also established criteria for determining in which state the original custody decision can be made. This prevents one spouse from taking a child out of the home and moving to another state in an attempt to improve the chances of obtaining custody.

In a further attempt to prevent childnapping, the federal government also enacted the Parental Kidnappng Prevention Act. This law provided criminal penalties for kidnapping, established a federal parent-locator service, and required states to recognize and enforce custody decisions made in other states.

What Should You Do If Your Ex-Spouse Kidnaps Your Child?

If your ex-spouse takes your child or children, you should immediately take the following steps:

1. Report the abduction to your local police and ask them to place a description of your children and your ex-spouse and any other relevant information (such as the make, model, and license-plate number of your ex-spouse's car) into the Federal Bureau of Investigation's National Crime Information Center computer. This information then will become available all over the country.

2. Call the National Center for Missing and Exploited Children at (800) 843-5678. This organization can refer you to local support groups and can provide a wealth of detailed information on what you should do and where you can turn for help.

3. If the abduction takes place during your separation period and before a court has awarded custody, you should instruct your attorney to immediately begin custody proceedings.

4. You should contact your local police department or district attorney's office to press criminal charges. If your ex-spouse has fled to another state, a fugitive warrant can be issued and the FBI can become involved.

5. Obtain a number of certified copies of your custody decree. You must send copies to the family court and police department of the city or town in which your child or children eventually are located.

6. If the police in that city or town are reluctant to act, you should retain an attorney in that location to immediately obtain a court order.

7. After your child or children are returned, you should petition your local court to order supervised visitation or any other steps necessary to prevent a repeat kidnapping.

PROTECT YOURSELF AND YOUR CHILDREN BY ENFORCING CHILD-SUPPORT ORDERS

Studies have shown that as much as one-third of all court-ordered child support, about $4 billion, goes unpaid each year. Fortunately, the federal government and all state governments have passed several pieces of legislation that will make it increasingly difficult for noncustodial parents to evade their responsibilities. These key laws, which include the federal Child Support Enforcement Amendments of 1984, the Family Support Act of 1988, and the Revised Uniform Reciprocal Enforcement of Support Act, require that:

- Every state must establish a parent-locator service to assist in locating parents owing child support.
- The attorney general of each state must offer collection assistance, including serving papers on the parent, working out payment schedules, and, as a last resort, jailing the

parent. If the nonpaying parent has moved out of state, the attorney general's office must help the other parent in location and collection.

- Tax refunds, Social Security benefits, federal pensions, and other benefits are intercepted or garnished to make up arrears.
- Child-support obligations are not dischargeable through bankruptcy proceedings.
- By 1994, every state must enact laws mandating that all court-ordered child-support payments are deducted directly from a parent's wages unless that right is specifically waived by the custodial parent.
- By 1995, all states must develop automatic tracking and monitoring systems for parents not paying support.

If you are not receiving the child support ordered by the court, you should immediately contact the court that issued the order. You also should immediately contact your state child-support enforcement office. Your local family court clerk should be able to provide you with the number, or you can obtain:

▶ **Booklet:** *Handbook on Child Support Enforcement*
Cost: Free
Contains: A list of state enforcement offices, step-by-step procedures for obtaining a court order of support and enforcing that order, and a section for keeping records of payments.
From: Consumer Information Center
Pueblo, CO 81009

Another important information resource is:

▶ **List:** *Addresses and services of child-support advocacy groups*
Cost: Free, with self-addressed, stamped envelope
From: Children's Foundation—Child Support Project
815 15th Street, NW, Suite 928
Washington, DC 20005

You also will find valuable information in:

▶ **Handbook:** *The Custody Handbook: A Woman's Guide to Child Custody Disputes*
Cost: $7.95 postpaid
Contains: Covers every step in the custody-determination process, including appeals of unfavorable decisions
From: Women's Legal Defense Fund
2000 P Street, NW, Suite 400
Washington, DC 20036
(202) 887-0364

PROTECT YOURSELF BY ENFORCING ALIMONY ORDERS

Nonpayment of court-ordered alimony is also a common and serious problem. Because such payments often are vital in the process of getting back on one's feet financially, federal and state laws accord such obligations a special status. Alimony payments cannot be discharged through bankruptcy. Alimony and child-support arrears are the only debts that the federal government will collect through deductions from Social Security benefit checks. Courts also will help to collect back payments by ordering garnishment of wages and through a variety of other remedies.

One important step to ensure that you will receive all the alimony payments to which you are entitled is to act quickly when your ex-spouse falls behind in payments. You can obtain information on how you can proceed by contacting the clerk of the court that issued your divorce decree.

10

Protect Yourself When You Remarry

KEY FACTS

- The divorce rate for remarriages is higher than the divorce rate among couples marrying for the first time.
- Remarriages are much more likely to end with the death of one spouse.
- Remarriage can result in the loss of significant benefits, such as alimony payments and the right to collect Social Security benefits on an ex-spouse's earnings record.

According to the National Center for Health Statistics, more than 3 out of 4 divorced men and 2 out of 3 divorced women eventually remarry. In almost 4 out of every 10 weddings performed in the United States each year, either the bride or groom or both have been married before.

All these people remarry with the hope and the belief that love can be more wonderful the second time around. The facts are, however, that remarriages are more likely than first marriages to end in divorce. The average duration of a remarriage before divorce is 4.3 years, compared with seven years for first marriages. Remarriages also are much more likely to end with the death of one spouse.

These statistics emphasize a critical point: You should be even more careful to protect yourself (and your children) both legally and financially before and during a remarriage. Chances are that both of you have greater assets and liabilities than you did when you married for the first time. Among these assets could be important benefits that you will lose the moment you say "I do."

PROTECT YOURSELF WITH A PRENUPTIAL AGREEMENT

A prenuptial agreement is a necessity when you are remarrying. Before you begin the process of negotiating an agreement with your future spouse, you should carefully read Chapter 1 of this book. In addition, you should pay special attention to the following benefits you may lose when you remarry:

1. Alimony. In almost all cases, alimony payments permanently cease when you remarry. Although you certainly hope that your new marriage will last forever, you must consider the possibility that this marriage will end in divorce, with no guarantee that you will be granted alimony from your second spouse.

2. Social Security. If your previous marriage lasted ten years, you retained the right to collect retirement and disability benefits based on the earnings record of your ex-spouse. You permanently lose that right when you remarry. If you have not qualified for benefits on your own and your second marriage ends in divorce in less than ten years, you will not be eligible for Social Security or free Medicare Part A benefits.

3. Health insurance. Federal law requires that your ex-spouse's employer offers you the opportunity to remain on that company's health-insurance plan at group rates for three years after the end of your marriage. That right ends with your remarriage.

4. Life insurance. Your divorce settlement may require your ex-spouse to maintain life insurance with you as the beneficiary. That obligation normally ends with remarriage.

5. Taxes. Your right to file tax returns as a Qualifying Widow or Widower or Head of Household ends with your remarriage.

If any of these situations affect you, you must discuss them thoroughly with your attorney and, perhaps, a financial planner or other professional. You must develop a plan to protect yourself from the possibly catastrophic results of losing your Social Security benefits or other assets. The best way to protect yourself is through the provisions of a prenuptial agreement that require your spouse to transfer sufficient property or maintain sufficient life insurance to provide financial needs for you in the event of a divorce. The prenuptial agreement also can require your spouse to maintain health and other insurance coverage that you are losing.

PROTECT YOURSELF FINANCIALLY DURING REMARRIAGE

Before you remarry, you should review the information about protecting your assets and property as discussed in Chapter 2. You likely have accumulated valuable property before your marriage. The first step in protecting your assets is through a comprehensive and valid prenuptial agreement. Then during marriage, you should:

1. Take care to keep your separate property separate. Don't commingle your funds with marital property and do carefully document any funds you contribute to the purchase of marital assets.

2. Limit your liability to joint debts. If your joint property is not sufficient to cover joint debts, a creditor has the legal right to pursue your separate property. You should be careful about joint credit cards, joint personal credit lines, cosigning business loans, and other actions that could place your assets at risk.

3. Become actively involved in managing your finances on a day-to-day basis. The best protection against financial surprises is establishing and following a household budget and maintaining a complete financial-records file.

PROTECT YOUR CHILDREN DURING REMARRIAGE

Almost one in four American children will live in a household with a stepparent at some point before reaching adulthood. In most cases, remarriage has a positive effect on these children. However, you should protect your children by:

1. Ensuring their right to inherit your property through a valid prenuptial agreement.

2. Protecting child-support payments. Remarriage does not end your ex-spouse's obligation to continue child support. Courts also will refuse to lower child-support payments simply because your financial condition improved through remarriage. You should be just as vigorous in collecting child-support payments as you were when you were single.

However, you should carefully document how these child-support funds are spent. You want to eliminate any suggestion that you or your new spouse are misusing these funds.

3. Retain control over your children's finances. As explained in detail in Chapter 3, you and your spouse are entitled to any wages earned by your minor children. But you are required to manage all of their other funds, such as inheritances, in trust for them. Most experts recommend that you, rather than the stepparent, manage these funds. This removes both the temptation for and the appearance of mismanagement.

4. Be even more vigilant about protecting yourself and your children against domestic violence and abuse. Statistically, these crimes are more common in households where one or both spouses have remarried. For more information, read Chapter 6.

PROTECT YOURSELF THROUGH ESTATE PLANNING

Becoming a widow or widower is a very unpleasant thought, but you must overcome this unpleasantness to effectively plan for that eventuality. To protect yourself, you should:

1. Settle questions of inheritance of separate property in a prenuptial agreement. The longer you wait, the more likely that your spouse's other heirs will challenge your rights.

2. Rewrite both of your wills immediately after remarriage. If you don't have wills, remarriage makes them more necessary than ever. A prenuptial agreement alone is not sufficient protection that your property, your spouse's property, and your marital property will be distributed exactly in accordance with your wishes.

3. Make sure that you are officially named as the beneficiary of all life insurance policies, annuities, pension plans, and other assets to which you and your spouse agree you are entitled. If you are the beneficiary, these assets pass to you without going through probate court.

4. Make sure that your spouse has elected the joint-survivor benefit for all vested pension plans and that you have been properly recorded as spouse.

5. Consult a financial professional about the estate-planning implications of all major purchases and financial decisions. In a remarriage, such decisions regarding exactly how property will be held are even more important.

6. Consult an attorney who can advise you and your spouse about drawing up living wills and durable powers of attorney. These documents provide protection if you or your spouse becomes unable to make decisions about your health care and becomes unable to handle your finances.

11

Know Your Rights as a Widow or Widower

KEY FACTS

- Nine out of ten women will become widows and one out of six men will become widowers.
- Federal law provides significant consumer protection during the difficult and emotional process of planning a funeral.
- A spouse cannot be disinherited unless he or she has waived inheritance rights in a valid prenuptial agreement.
- State laws protect your home and several other assets from the creditors of your deceased spouse.
- Support groups can provide enormous help in overcoming grief and coping with the practical problems of getting on with your life.

For most women, losing a spouse is almost a certainty. Many of the steps you can take to protect yourself begin with a prenuptial agreement and continue into the marriage with such activities as money management, estate planning, preparation of a will, and protecting Social Security and pension benefits. Additional information, however, becomes important at that very difficult time when a spouse passes away.

PROTECT YOURSELF WHILE ARRANGING YOUR SPOUSE'S FUNERAL

After the death of a spouse, the first task that must be faced is planning a funeral and burial. In response to many complaints about deceptive funeral practices, the Federal Trade Commission instituted a funeral-industry trade regulation in 1984. Among other things, this regulation requires that:

- All funeral providers must give detailed price information over the telephone, allowing comparison shopping.
- All funeral providers must provide you with a detailed written price list.
- All funeral providers may not falsely state that embalming is required by law and must disclose in writing that you have the right to choose alternatives, such as direct burial or cremation.
- All funeral providers must disclose in writing any charges for arranging purchases, such as flowers, newspaper obituaries, etc.
- All funeral providers may not tell you that state or local law requires purchase of a casket for cremation.
- All funeral providers must disclose in writing that you have the right to choose only the funeral goods and services that you want.
- All funeral providers must give you an itemized statement of all charges after you make your selection of the products and services.

For further information or to register complaints:

- **Publication:** *Consumer Guide to the FTC Funeral Rule*
  Cost: Free
  From: Federal Trade Commission
  Bureau of Consumer Protection
  Washington, DC 20580

Among the other important sources of information about funeral planning are:

- **Book:** *It's Your Choice*
  Cost: $4.95 ($3.00 to AARP members) plus $1.75 postage
  Contains: A complete manual of funeral planning
  From: AARP Books/Scott, Foresman and Co.
  1865 Miner Street
  Des Plaines, IL 60016

- **Organization:** National Funeral Directors Association
  Services: This association provides two important consumer services. First, it issues a wide variety of free publications, including:
  - *Anatomical Gifts*
  - *Cremation*
  - *Death Away from Home*
  - *Easing the Burden*
  - *Embalming*
  - *Funerals Are for the Living*
  - *Funeral Costs*
  - *Funeral Etiquette*
  - *Grief*
  - *Helping Groups*
  - *In Service of Others*

- *Living When Your Spouse Has Died*
- *Living with Dying*
- *Suicide*
- *The Traditional Funeral*
- *A Way to Remember*
- *What Are My Options?*
- *What Can I Do to Help?*
- *When Death Occurs*
- *When Your Parent Dies*
- *Will I Ever Stop Hurting?*

The second service is the Funeral Service Consumer Arbitration Board, which mediates disputes between individuals and funeral providers.

For publications: NFDA Learning Resources Center
1121 West Oklahoma Avenue
Milwaukee, WI 53227
(414) 541-2500

For arbitration: Funeral Service Consumer Arbitration Program
PO Box 27641
Milwaukee, WI 53227
(800) 662-7666

▶ **Organization:** Cremation Association of North America
111 East Wacker Drive
Chicago, IL 60601
(312) 644-6610

Services: Provides the following publications (with self-addressed envelope stamped with $ .50)

- *Cremation Explained*
- *Choices to Make Now for the Future*
- *Cremation Is Not the End*
- *So You've Chosen Cremation*
- *Cremation Memorials*

▶ **Organization:** Continental Association of Funeral and Memorial Societies
2001 South Street, NW, Suite 530
Washington, DC 20009
(202) 745-0634

Services: Disseminates information about alternatives for funeral planning. Provides information and referral to "memorial societies," nonprofit groups that arrange for low-cost funeral services to members.

▶ **Organization:** The U.S. Department of Veterans Affairs
Services: All veterans of military service are entitled to a burial plot in a federal cemetery, a marker for the grave, and an American flag for the casket. The families of all deceased veterans also are eligible for a small burial allowance.
For information: Contact the nearest VA office (see your telephone directory listing, "U.S. Government").

PROTECT YOURSELF IF YOUR SPOUSE DIED WITHOUT A WILL

As explained in Chapter 4, certain property that you and your spouse held jointly, such as bank accounts and title to your home, pass automatically to you on your spouse's death. If your spouse died without a will, however, all other property will be divided according to your state's intestate succession law. The laws of every state provide for a minimum of one-third to one-half share to be distributed to the surviving spouse. The disposition of the rest of the estate depends on the number of children and other close relatives of your deceased spouse. If there were no children or close relatives, you would receive the entire estate.

Most state laws also provide for a surviving spouse to receive a fair share of the property that is not included in the estate. For example, your ex-spouse may have owned a business or real estate jointly with a third party. Because this ownership in effect disinherited the surviving spouse, these laws allow the surviving spouse to "elect" to take a share of such property in lieu of the surviving spouse's share of the estate under the intestate succession laws.

It is difficult for a nonprofessional to make the right decisions when a spouse dies without a will. Therefore, you should protect yourself by retaining the services of an attorney who specializes in wills and estates.

PROTECT YOURSELF IF YOUR SPOUSE ATTEMPTED TO DISINHERIT YOU

The laws in every state invalidate any will in which the spouse is disinherited, with the following exceptions:

- The surviving spouse waived all claims to the estate in a valid prenuptial agreement.
- The surviving spouse was guilty of proven desertion or other serious marital misconduct.

If any relative or any other party makes any attempt to interfere with your right to inherit, you should consult an attorney.

PROTECT YOURSELF FROM YOUR DECEASED SPOUSE'S CREDITORS

Almost every state has enacted homestead laws, which are designed to ensure that the family has a place to live after the death of a spouse. These laws exempt residences and certain personal property from claims by creditors. The only exceptions are residences with mortgage agreements also signed by surviving spouses and liens for back real estate taxes.

Most states also have additional exempt property laws that establish certain amounts and types of property that can be distributed to the surviving spouse and heirs free from claims by the deceased spouse's creditors.

For information about both the homestead-exemption and exempt-property laws, you should consult an attorney.

PROTECT YOURSELF BY CONTACTING SUPPORT GROUPS

Among the resources for widowed persons are:

▸ **Organization:** Widowed Persons Service
AARP
1909 K Street, NW
Washington, DC 20049

Services: Social outreach and support service for widows and widowers organized by AARP

▸ **Publication:** *On Being Alone: A Guide for Widowed Persons*
Cost: Free
From: AARP
1909 K Street, NW
Washington, DC 20049

▸ **Publication:** *Final Details: A Guide for Survivors When Death Occurs*
Cost: Free
Contains: Four-page fact sheets for each of the 50 states, prepared by AARP
From: AARP
1909 K Street, NW
Washington, DC 20049

▸ **Publications:** *Survival Handbook for Widows* ($6.95, $4.95 for AARP members, plus $1.75 postage), *Alone—Not Lonely; Independent Living for Women over Fifty* ($6.95, $4.95 for AARP members, plus $1.75 postage)
From: AARP Books/Scott Foresman and Co.
1865 Miner Street
Des Plaines, IL 60016

- **Publication:** *What Do You Do Now?*
  Cost: $1.30
  From: Life Insurance Marketing and Research Association
  PO Box 208
  Hartford, CT 06141

- **Organization:** The Theos Foundation
  Penn Hills Mall, Suite 410
  Pittsburgh, PA 15235
  (412) 243-4299
  Services: Referral to local sources of financial and emotional counsel for widows and widowers

- **Organization:** Your local area agency on aging
  Services: Many area agencies provide special counseling and bereavement programs for widows and widowers
  For information: Your local area agency on aging

- **Organization:** Your local senior center
  Services: Most senior centers also provide special counseling and bereavement programs
  For information: See your telephone directory or call your local area agency on aging

Index

0852